Praise for *From One Stage to Another*

"A fascinating story of a real-life pop star who became a transformative leader."

—**Rusty Komori**, bestselling author of *Superior*

"Glenn Medeiros' inspirational story as a singing idol reflects his character and ambition; he's also a compassionate hyphenate who excels in life—as a son, student, teacher, father, husband, educator, and now, author."

—**Wayne Harada**, retired columnist,
The Honolulu Advertiser

"Watching Glenn rise from Brown Bags to international success was unforgettable. His story shows that fame was only the beginning—his greatest legacy is how he continues to inspire Hawai'i and beyond."

—**Brook Lee**, Miss Universe 1997

From One Stage to Another

Lessons Learned in Music, Education, and Leadership

Glenn Medeiros, Ed. D.

MADE FOR SUCCESS

Made for Success Publishing
www.MadeForSuccess.com

Distributed by Made for Success

First Printing

Library of Congress Cataloging-in-Publication data
Medeiros, Glenn, Ed. D.
From One Stage to Another: Lessons Learned in Music, Education, and Leadership
p. cm.

LCCN: 2025943979
ISBN: 978-1-64146-960-9 *(Hardcover)*
ISBN: 978-1-64146-961-6 *(eBook)*
ISBN: 978-1-64146-962-3 *(Audio)*

Printed in the United States of America

For further information, contact Made for Success Publishing
email service@madeforsuccess.net.

This book is dedicated to my parents,
Robert and Dorothy Medeiros.
Your example of unconditional love,
dedication to family, hard work,
and faith in the Lord has made all the difference.

Contents

FOREWORD BY ELSA LUNGHINI

French singer and actress who rose to fame in the 1980s, enchanting European audiences with her chart-topping duet "Un Roman d'amitié" ("A Friendship Story")—a memorable collaboration with a young Glenn Medeiros.

Our first steps toward each other were shy, but very quickly we recognized ourselves in one another. Together, we could be carefree, free, and above all, ourselves. We experienced success from a very young age, and the sense of freedom we felt as we navigated this new success as a duo brought us much joy, lightness, and comfort.

Our moods resonated with each other. It gave us extra strength to face the whirlwind that swept us up. Although our backgrounds were different, we spoke the same language.

He was my friend, my confidant. The thread that connected me to my adolescence. A true, sincere friendship that found its place with ease and naturalness.

Glenn was very funny. I remember contagious, difficult-to-repress laughter. Kindness was also one of his great qualities. I have rarely met someone in my artistic life who was as kind and attentive. He was very attentive, considerate, and aware of others despite his young age and fame.

During our "Friendship Story," we lived an extraordinary moment—filled with travel, sharing, and adrenaline.

Returning to our respective countries was a feared and painful moment. We knew that our professional projects and the physical distance between us would inevitably cause a rupture.

We gradually drifted apart, but those memories remain vivid and happy, even after several decades.

An enchanting chapter of a piece of adolescence.

I know that music has always been and will always be an integral part of his life, and I can only admire the path he has taken so far—a radical, courageous, and well-deserved career change.

Elsa Lunghini,
Singer and actress

PRÉFACE

Comme de nombreuses jeunes filles de 14 ans en 1987, la chanson « Nothing's gonna change my love for you » et le sourire de Glenn étaient une bouffée d'air frais dans le paysage musical. Notre rencontre fut arrangée par nos producteurs respectifs de l'époque, qui voyaient en nous une association artistique prometteuse.

Les premiers pas l'un vers l'autre furent timides mais très rapidement nous nous sommes reconnus l'un et l'autre, l'un chez l'autre. Nous pouvions être, ensemble, insouciants, libres et surtout nous-même. Nous vivions le succès chacun de notre côté à un très jeune âge et le sentiment de liberté que nous éprouvions en traversant ce nouveau succès en duo nous apportait beaucoup de joie, de légèreté et de réconfort.

Nos états d'âme résonnaient chez l'autre. Ça nous donnait une force supplémentaire pour affronter le tourbillon qui nous happait. Bien que nos cultures fussent différentes, nous parlions la même langue.

C'était mon ami, mon confident. Le fil d'Ariane qui me reliait à mon adolescence. Une amitié vraie, sincère qui avait trouvé sa place avec beaucoup d'aisance et d'évidence.

Glenn était très drôle. Je me souviens de fous rire contagieux et très difficiles à réprimer. La gentillesse était également une de ses grandes qualités. J'ai rarement côtoyé dans ma vie artistique quelqu'un d'aussi gentil et attentionné. Il était très à l'écoute, prévenant et conscient de l'autre malgré son jeune âge et sa notoriété.

Nous avons vécu, le temps de notre « Roman d'amitié », un moment de vie extraordinaire, empreint de voyages, de partages et d'adrénaline.

Le retour dans nos pays respectifs avait été un moment redouté et douloureux. Nous savions que nos projets professionnels et la distance physique qui s'imposaient à nous, allaient créer inévitablement une rupture.

Nous nous sommes éloignés petit à petit mais ces souvenirs restent vivaces et heureux, même après quelques décennies.

Une parenthèse enchantée d'un morceau d'adolescence.

Je sais que la musique fait et fera toujours partie intégrante de sa vie et je ne peux que saluer le chemin qu'il a parcouru jusqu'à aujourd'hui, une reconversion professionnelle radicale, courageuse et méritante.

Elsa Lunghini

PROLOGUE

People often say my life has taken an unexpected path. I started out as a shy kid in a small town on a tiny island in the middle of the Pacific Ocean, raised with modest means and big dreams. Somehow, that quiet beginning led me to stages around the world—singing internationally, selling millions of records, and meeting people I once only saw on TV. Every chapter of my journey brought new adventures and challenges I wasn't always ready for. This book is about those moments—both the triumphs and the lessons that came with them.

From my early days as a struggling student in elementary school to eventually earning a doctorate in Educational Leadership and serving as both a teacher and professor, my journey has been shaped by a wide range of experiences. Along the way, I've grown not only as a student but also as a performer, educator, and leader. Each role has offered its own obstacles, all of which have helped shape the person I am today. My hope is to share these experiences with you—offering honest reflections and meaningful insights that can positively impact you as you navigate your own path in life.

Throughout the various stages of my life, I was blessed with individuals who, in one way or another, provided me the knowledge I needed to reach my goals and aspirations while also providing me the strength I needed to weather turbulent times. These individuals were like guardian angels sent to me at the right time, in the right place, for the right reasons. I believe that all of us have these guardian angels. The challenge is to be aware of them and to learn from them.

On the other hand, life always seeks balance. With every success you achieve, challenges are sure to follow. While some people will support and uplift you, others may respond with jealousy or selfishness. These individuals may try to bring you down—not because of anything you've done wrong, but simply because your presence threatens their own ambitions. One of the most important lessons in life is learning how to protect your energy from these negative influences while also finding the strength to forgive them, as my faith teaches me.

Whether you're a student, educator, leader, artist, or simply someone navigating life's many paths, the lessons in this book are meant to offer guidance. I share insights from my own successes—and, just as importantly, from my mistakes—with the hope that they can help you make thoughtful choices in your own journey. More than just lessons, this book is also a collection of stories about the people I've met and the places I've been. I hope that, beyond any takeaways, you'll find these stories engaging and relatable.

So, wherever you are in life, I invite you to come along.

Chapter 1

EARLY INFLUENCES

My early childhood memories, though few, played a crucial role in shaping my views of myself, others, and the world. I grew up in a loving home with my mother always close by, tending to the house while my father worked tirelessly as a bus driver, day and night. Our home was often filled with the sounds of PBS shows like *Sesame Street* and *The Electric Company*. We spent hours playing board games, cards, and records on the phonograph, and I was captivated by Japanese children's programs on KIKU Television. This early exposure sparked my admiration for Japanese culture, with shows like *Ultra Seven* and *Kikaida* becoming my favorites, and I even learned to sing some of my first songs in Japanese.

My mother's passion for music was another significant influence. She had a beautiful voice and an ear for melody, and singing with her was one of my favorite activities. She introduced me to the magic of music, and Elvis Presley became my first musical inspiration. The little record player that we won at a fundraiser was a prized possession. We spent countless hours listening to records, singing along, and dancing around the living room.

After my grandfather lost his legs to diabetes, my mother stopped attending grade school to help support her family. She could read relatively well, but when it came to writing, she depended on my father for that. Despite her limited education, she was a source of endless support and wisdom. Her decision to leave school and help her family shaped her into a resilient and resourceful woman. She instilled in me the values of hard work, perseverance, and the importance of family.

My father, a graduate of Waimea High School in Kaua'i, was seldom home due to extra shifts to pay for our mortgage and essentials. His absence was a constant reminder of the sacrifices he made for us. The long hours he worked ensured that we had a roof over our heads and food on the table. His dedication and perseverance were inspiring, and I hoped as a child to be as hardworking and responsible as he was someday. He was a pillar of strength.

My parents provided me and my siblings with the essentials needed to live a good life, and my mother watched every penny. We did not have a lot of material things, but we had lots of love. I vividly recall my mother using food stamps at the grocery store and my father proudly bringing home pigs or deer he had hunted over the weekend. He would share his catch with our neighbors, reinforcing the sense of mutual support and camaraderie that defined our small town of Lāwaʻi.

The sense of community was particularly strong during our visits to the McBryde Sugar Plantation, where my mother had grown up. The sugar plantation parties were a celebration of life and culture. The food was a delightful mix of Portuguese, Puerto Rican, and Hawaiian cuisines, a testament to the diverse heritage of the plantation workers. The music, the laughter, and the camaraderie created an atmosphere of warmth and belonging. These gatherings were a reminder of the strength and resilience of our ancestors, who arrived in Hawaii from Portugal in the late 1800s and had built a life for themselves in a foreign land through hard work and unity.

Despite this loving environment, I recall the tension caused by our modest means. The financial strain was palpable. My mother maintained our home with unwavering dedication, rendering it a pristine sanctuary that was both inviting and somewhat daunting to navigate. Renowned in Lāwaʻi for her impeccable housekeeping, she saw cleanliness not as a chore but as a shield against chaos, a source of pride, and a pillar of structure. Alongside my older sister, they tirelessly polished every surface, leaving no corner untouched. While I came to admire their diligence, I confess I didn't contribute much to their efforts. In my mother's eyes, traditional roles were clear: men provided outside the home, while women tended to the home. Despite my offers, my help was kindly declined. I admired her dedication and learned the value of hard work and attention to detail.

Looking back, I realize how these formative years influenced my outlook on life. The financial challenges we faced taught me the importance of perseverance and the value of hard work. The love and support of my family provided a strong foundation that helped me navigate the ups and downs of life. The sense of community and the importance of sharing and supporting one another became integral to my identity. My parents ensured that we never felt deprived. They made the most of what we had, creating a nurturing environment. They taught us to appreciate the simple pleasures in life, like a home-cooked meal, a beautiful song, or attending Mass each Sunday. They showed us the importance of community, sharing, and supporting one another in times of need.

Our home, though modest, was a sanctuary of love and learning. The television shows we watched were more than mere entertainment; they were windows to the world beyond our small town. They taught me about different cultures, languages, and ways of thinking. They sparked my curiosity and fueled my imagination. I often found myself lost in daydreams, inspired by the stories and characters I saw on the screen.

Chapter 2

AN OUTSIDER

Before attending kindergarten, my life was largely confined to our home. Outings were rare and driven by necessity, such as trips to the grocery store, church, the beach, or watching my older brother play sports. However, my parents had many siblings, and we often visited them, creating a sense of belonging. With many aunties and uncles and many more cousins, I was surrounded by much love and support, making me feel a strong sense of what we call "ohana" in Hawaii.

As kindergarten began, I soon realized that many of my new classmates had already attended preschool. While I am thankful for the television shows I watched in this early stage of my life and the information I gathered from them, little did I know that while I was at home learning what I could, many of my future classmates were already attending preschool at small private preschools on the island and were learning skills like writing letters and decoding the sounds of words. Even though this was a bit of a disadvantage for a young boy about to enter school with others who already had a year of learning under their belts, I never blamed my parents for not being able to afford preschool. My parents had given me something far more valuable than formal education—they had given me a loving home, a sense of belonging, and the resilience to overcome challenges. These early experiences laid the groundwork for my future, shaping me into the person I am today.

In retrospect, attending preschool would have greatly impacted my educational journey. A growing trend in Hawaii today is to expand preschool opportunities to as many children as possible. The habits and skills developed at a young age profoundly impact students' future academic success. For families who can't afford preschool, educational technology offers a solution. Interactive educational tools created by educators can teach young children to read and write, setting them on a path to success from the start. It's essential to foster good habits early because unlearning bad ones, like incorrect pencil grips, is much harder than learning them correctly the first time.

Preschool also helps create cognitive branches in the minds of young learners by exposing children to new experiences and places. This early exposure makes it easier for them to absorb and retain new information related to their past experiences when learning new concepts. While many of my classmates were well-prepared to enter kindergarten, my lack of such early preparation made my kindergarten year incredibly challenging.

When I started kindergarten, I lacked both a creative mind and the basic skills to express myself. At home, everything had been done for me, so I rarely learned from failure. The fear of making mistakes, especially in front of my peers, made school a nerve-wracking experience. This constant anxiety made my kindergarten year challenging, leaving my self-efficacy for learning seriously hampered for many years. My first day of school was particularly impactful, and I want to share this experience in detail to help others understand the thoughts and feelings some children have when starting school. Understanding this can highlight a single day's lasting impact on a child's self-perception.

My first day in kindergarten began with the distinct smell of new clothes, fresh from the pages of the Sears catalog my parents had meticulously ordered from. We seldom shopped for clothing, unable to afford what we considered "nice clothes." Unlike the usual T-shirts, shorts, and slippers I wore daily, my mother had a tradition each summer: she took my measurements and ordered five sets of matching shirts and pants, along with a new pair of shoes that had to be black. She believed other colors would show the daily wear and tear too quickly, knowing we would not be able to purchase shoes again until the following year. Although I wasn't fond of black shoes, I was thrilled to have new ones for my first day of school.

Walking to the bus stop, I got a taste of the day ahead when the neighborhood kids, who had never seen me dressed up, teased, "Hey, Glenn. Nice shirt and pants, brah! Thought you guys didn't have money!" Unlike me, they were content in their everyday attire of kamaboko slippers, surf shorts, and T-shirts. As we waited for the bus, I noticed most girls were dressed up, some even with makeup, contrasting sharply with the boys' casual outfits.

When I boarded the bus, I faced another obstacle: where to sit. Almost everyone seemed to have their preferred spots. I chose a seat at the front to avoid the rowdy eighth graders at the back who were yelling, using vulgar language, and sometimes teasing others.

Arriving at school was an overwhelming experience. It was my first time on campus, and I had no idea where to go or what to do. Most students were dropped off by their parents, but my mother, plagued by chronic motion sickness, rarely drove. Gasoline expenses also made driving impractical. My older siblings took a different bus to their high school in Lihue, twenty minutes away from where I attended school in Koloa, leaving me alone in this new environment.

Lost and scared, I decided to follow kids who looked my age walking with their parents. I couldn't read the classroom names, so I aimlessly wandered, hoping to find my destination. Eventually, I stumbled upon my classroom, but I was already late. The other students were seated, busily writing their names and drawing pictures on worksheets. The day had barely begun, and I already felt out of place.

When my new teacher first saw me, I could see the frustration on her face. Her voice dripped with sarcasm as she pointed me to a desk and dropped a worksheet in front of me. Students were already settled to my left and right, and their school materials, backpacks, and other belongings were on their desks. It seemed they were being assigned cubby holes for their things. The teacher then instructed me to write my name in the top right corner of the document she handed me. This worksheet, destined for display at the front of my cubby hole, was a task I needed to catch up on, with several students having completed it.

Sweat began to roll down my face, not just from the frantic search for my classroom but from the anxiety of the moment. I had no idea how to write my name, let alone hold a pencil correctly. What happened next would haunt me for years. The teacher, noticing my struggle, peered at my paper with a mix of confusion and irritation before announcing loudly, "What's wrong with you? You don't even know how to write your name?" It took every ounce of willpower not to cry. Eventually, I managed to scrawl my name, but it was a messy first attempt. For the rest of the year, that poorly written name in front of my cubby hole was a constant reminder of my shaky start.

Later that day, the teacher asked me to line up next to her desk with a few other students. Out of the thirty or so in class, only four of us had been singled out. She told us to walk to the office to collect our tokens for lunch. At the time, I didn't even know what a token was. Later, I discovered that, like the other three students, I qualified for free lunch and had to stand in a long line each day at the office to get my lunch tokens. Standing in that line on the first day and every day after was a humiliating experience. I never complained to my parents because I knew they were doing their best, but I made it my mission to ensure no one saw me in that line.

When we finally returned to class with our tokens, I was once again behind. The next lesson had already begun, leaving me scrambling to catch up.

Unfortunately, this sense of falling behind, feeling lost, afraid, different, or less than, clung to me throughout my school years. Most of my classmates had already formed tight-knit friendships with peers they had known since preschool. Meanwhile, I carried my pencils and materials in a plain brown bag, while my classmates had cool-looking backpacks and stylish pencil boxes brimming with expensive pens and pencils.

Each day after school, I returned home on the bus, eagerly anticipating the comforting sight of my mother. I remember telling her that I didn't like my teacher very much. She offered to speak with her, but the thought of potentially getting into an argument with my mother was something I did not want for me, my mother, or my teacher, so I quickly said no.

Schoolwork continued to be a struggle for me. It usually took me longer to finish assignments compared to my classmates. Homework, in particular, was a struggle because of my busy after-school schedule. I had already started playing t-ball and Pee Wee football, driven by my desire to impress my father, who was a big fan of those sports. My father was a man of few words, but sports were a surefire way to draw him into a conversation. Although I never became the athlete my father envisioned, sports introduced me to friends and kept me safe from bullies who knew I could hold my own on the field despite being quiet and shy. This helped me make friends in school but hurt me when it came to completing homework.

As a result, I started, at a very young age, rushing through assignments without putting in the time and effort needed to produce quality work. No one at home could help me with the work I didn't understand. I became content with completing work at a satisfactory level as long as it didn't take too much time. Besides not putting forth my best effort, I often needed clarification about the instructions I received at school. Speaking a rigid type of Pidgin English at home made it difficult for me to express myself using proper grammar, both verbally and in writing, in school.

Furthermore, most of the instruction I received involved listening to a long series of steps that I was required to follow. Having had very little practice at home listening to instructions and following through, I needed to gain the skills to break down information into bite-sized pieces that I could remember, understand, file appropriately in my mind, and easily retrieve when required. Once I began reading in school, I had a difficult time with something called saliency determination. I tried remembering everything I read instead of focusing on the main points, which often led to cognitive overload. It was challenging even if I scheduled time to do my homework because no one could help me with it. My brother was out playing sports, and my mother and sister were constantly cleaning, creating a poor environment for studying. Ultimately, I had many excuses for my lack of effort, but I was solely to blame for giving less than my best during this stage of my life.

There were several factors that played a role in my lack of success in school. I didn't believe in myself or my academic abilities or value education enough to make the sacrifices needed for improvement. This lack of emphasis on education stemmed from my family life. The importance of attaining a solid education leading to college was never discussed in our household. My parents wanted us to have faith in God, treat others well, find decent jobs, get married, buy a modest home, and raise a family. In retrospect, there's nothing inherently wrong with that, but for many of my classmates and their parents, going to college was the target from day one, and much of their time was spent helping their kids eventually reach that goal.

Most of my friends were of Asian descent, and attaining success in school was their highest priority. Everything else seemed to take a back seat. The majority of people in Hawaii are at least part Asian, and most of my teachers were of Japanese-American descent. Teaching was held in high esteem among Japanese-American families in Hawaii. As one of my Japanese mentors once told me, "If you were Japanese in Hawaii and male, you were encouraged to study engineering. On the other hand, if you were female, the most honorable job was to be a school teacher." There were teachers in school from various ethnic backgrounds, but most of the teachers at the elementary school I attended in Koloa were of Japanese descent. This led me to associate great intelligence with those who were Asian-American, which, since I am not, left me feeling less intelligent.

My teachers spent a lot of time exposing us to Japanese culture through poetry, such as haikus, pictures, films, and many books. We read and analyzed books like *Momotaro* repeatedly in our language arts classes. At the time, I thought my teachers favored studying their own culture over others, but as an educator today, I understand that many other factors were at play.

Given that they are most familiar with their cultural values and practices, it's only natural that they teach using different aspects of them. I could see my Japanese-American classmates bonding more closely with my teachers. Now, I realize that it's not unusual for people to be naturally attracted to each other when they share similar cultural practices and beliefs. Nonetheless, these experiences in school gave me the perception that Asians were somehow cognitively superior and, therefore, reinforced my feelings of inadequacy and eroded my self-confidence. This false perception was further supported when I looked around the neighborhood and saw the stark differences in the types of houses, cars, and jobs Asian Americans had compared to Portuguese families like mine.

Then, a teacher entered my life that literally changed my trajectory. He was, by far, one of the best teachers I had. He was my baseball coach, Mr. Sakimai. For some reason, this Japanese-American coach treated me like I was extra special, even though my baseball skills were average at best. It took some time for me to get used to it. I remember him going out of his way to ensure all players on our team had the opportunity to try out for each position on the field. He seemed more concerned with the character of his players rather than winning or losing. Our team did pretty well, and at the end of the season, he took me aside one day after practice and told me that I was selected to be an alternate on the all-star team that would travel to Honolulu to play some of the best teams within our age bracket. That meant the world to me! I had only been off the island of Kaua'i once, and being chosen for the all-star team gave a massive lift to my confidence and made my father beam with pride.

Mr. Sakimai was one of the first educators God brought into my life who helped me create a more positive perception of myself. I will never forget the lesson he taught me about the importance of educators conveying that they see greatness in all their students. Most of my teachers may have seen all their students as having the same potential, but the opposite message was often received. But Mr. Sakimai was different; he saw greatness in all his students; he was the first teacher to say, "I believe in you," four seemingly small words that have a giant impact!

As I got a little older, I began spending more time outside of my home with kids in my neighborhood. The house we lived in would be considered middle-class by today's standards. A few of my neighbors were doctors and engineers, but most worked in public service jobs or were blue-collar workers.

After years of living in the little town of Lāwaʻi, elementary school became a gateway to a new world full of opportunities to meet like-minded friends. Every Wednesday, the Catholic kids from Koloa School would hop on a bus to attend Catechism classes, returning just before the school day ended. I was drawn to a group of kids who participated in those Wednesday classes and began attending with them. The friendships I formed during those Catechism sessions have stood the test of time; some of those friends remain my closest companions to this day. Our bond was forged through shared faith and a mutual love for music. Despite being the only non-Filipino in the group, a common bond was created as many of the kids also grew up on a plantation like many of my family members did.

Exposure to different perspectives at a young age is crucial for shaping a child's mind, and this was certainly true for me. While I noticed that others often had more material possessions, I never felt envious. Instead, I celebrated their successes, attributing them to hard work—a value I've always admired and continue to hold dear.

My early school experiences shed light on an important issue: many children start school unprepared, and educators need to be aware of this. Teachers constantly send messages through their actions and words, which students interpret based on their unique backgrounds. The challenges students face sometimes have little to do with teacher performance but can significantly influence the learning environment. When teachers focus on each student's strengths, regardless of the challenges they bring from home, it can boost their confidence and help them view themselves more positively.

At the school where I serve as president, we create a special "First Day of School" experience for kindergarteners. It allows parents to walk their children to class and meet their teachers, ensuring a safe and caring first impression. Schools should be places where mistakes are valued as steps toward solving problems, diversity is celebrated, and students' strengths are as important as their areas for growth. Although my own school journey was challenging and set the tone for my later years, I hold no grudges. The teachers I had were dedicated individuals doing their best. Ironically, my negative experiences in elementary school motivated me to eventually become an educator. One of my goals as an educator is to create a nurturing learning environment for all students in my care, similar to the one my baseball coach, Mr. Sakimai, fostered on the field.

Chapter 3

POCHO KID

During my later childhood, I found myself yearning to acquire specific skills, driven by a desire to carve out my own place in the world. I longed to feel truly loved and appreciated beyond the unconditional love my family had already provided. Though I had a small group of friends from my neighborhood, church, and school, I did not stand out in a crowd. I was the shy one, often seen as someone who didn't take school too seriously, enjoyed sports, but mostly just wanted to have fun and take things easy.

Night after night, I would lose myself in music on my Walkman, letting the melodies lull me to sleep. Even at a young age, I was a romantic, dreamily listening to lyrics that spoke to the feelings I didn't yet fully understand. Deep down, I knew I had a gift—a singing voice that could captivate—but fear kept me from sharing it with the world. Instead, I convinced myself that earning respect as an athlete, as most of my friends did, was the right path. Despite knowing I was a better singer than an athlete, the idea of performing on stage terrified me. So, I poured my energy into sports, hoping it might fill the void left by the talent I was too afraid to showcase.

Growing up, I was an average athlete, capable of holding my own on the field, but it was the love of the game that really fueled me. Initially, my motivation stemmed mostly from a desire to impress my father. We didn't spend much time together except on Sundays, at games, at the beach, in church, or during late-night dinners after practices. My older brother was a natural athlete. My father would tell me stories about my brother's potential in football and baseball, so it's no surprise that I tried hard to follow in my brother's footsteps, always striving to emulate him.

It wasn't about competition; I held a great deal of love and respect for my brother. But deep down, I wanted to earn the same kind of admiration from my father. I tried everything—playing football, baseball, and even learning to bat left-handed because my dad said it would get me closer to first base. That habit stuck, and to this day, I prefer swinging left-handed, whether it's a bat or a golf club. But despite my efforts, my dad never seemed overly impressed.

After games, I'd eagerly ask, "Dad, did you see da ball I caught today?"

His usual response was a casual, "Well, if you touch 'em, you should catch 'em, right?"

The thing is, I loved playing football. I was good enough to start on offense and defense, but I lacked the work ethic and confidence to truly excel. My experiences with baseball, soccer, and martial arts were all pretty similar. Fortunately, there came a point when I began to shift my focus from sports to music. But the big question loomed: how could I find the courage to sing in front of my peers? I feared being ridiculed by my friends and had no idea how they would react. The thought of stepping onto a stage to share my voice was terrifying, yet the attraction of music was too strong to ignore.

One of my classmates at Koloa Elementary School was a boy named Michael, a fun-loving, energetic kid who had a knack for getting into trouble with the teachers. One teacher, in particular, was Mr. Arnold Meister, who taught both science and music. Mr. Meister was no ordinary teacher—he was an accomplished actor, singer, and songwriter from Texas who chose to make Kaua'i his home for reasons I'll never fully understand. I had always felt he belonged on Broadway, sharing his talent with the world. Nonetheless, he dedicated himself to teaching full-time while still pursuing his passion for performing on a part-time basis.

Michael was the most talented actor in our class, and Mr. Meister recognized this, even going so far as to write an original musical with Michael as one of the leads. Determined to make the show a success, Michael made sure everyone was giving their best in singing, dancing, and acting. I was one of the quietest kids in class at the time, but one day, as Michael stood next to me, I found the courage to sing a little louder in front of my classmates. I'll never forget the look of surprise on Michael's face. He did a double-take and then shouted out to our teacher, "Mr. Meister! Mr. Meister! You gotta listen to Glenn. The buggah can sing good!" Before I knew it, Michael was dragging me toward the piano where Mr. Meister was playing. "Glenn! Sing for Mr. Meister! You gotta sing for him!" Michael insisted. My heart pounded as my classmates gathered around the piano, but I began to sing. At first, as did my classmates, Mr. Meister seemed a little surprised. But as I continued, some of them even began to cheer me on. After class, Mr. Meister approached me and said, "Glenn, I've got a role for you in this play." The news spread quickly; before I knew it, within a month of performing in the play, I had gone from being one of the quiet kids to being recognized as someone with a special talent.

After the musical, Mr. Meister saw something in me that I hadn't fully realized myself. He knew I needed to hone my talent if I wanted to pursue singing on stage. He offered to work with me after school, encouraging me to perform as a soloist and even lending me his keyboard to use at home, knowing my family couldn't afford one. When I was too scared to sing on stage alone for the first time, he cleverly paired me with my best friend, Pali Carbonel, knowing it would give me the confidence to perform. That small gesture made all the difference.

As I performed at various school events, I began to build a new sense of confidence in myself. It wasn't just about singing—it was about discovering a part of me that made me feel special and unique. While this newfound confidence didn't immediately translate to academics, it was a pivotal moment in my life. It was then that I decided I wanted to become an educator someday.

I had always respected teachers, but Mr. Meister's ability to take someone like me, who had very little self-confidence, and help me find and nurture my God-given talent was transformative. He inspired me to push past my fears and share my gift with the world. Although I knew I would pursue music, perhaps even professionally, what I wanted more was to become an educator, helping others discover their own potential just as Mr. Meister had done for me.

My mother always had a way of keeping my ego in check, especially when the compliments started pouring in after I began singing in school. From a young age, I knew I could always confide in her. Her advice was consistent—be kind to others and stay away from trouble. During one of our usual conversations at home, I suddenly realized that I hadn't seen my dad around the house for quite some time. I didn't think much of it at first, knowing he sometimes worked late shifts, picking up people from luau shows on his bus to earn extra money.

Eventually, my mother decided I was ready to hear the truth: my dad had been in the hospital for several days. She explained that he had suffered a nervous breakdown after being caught in a relationship with another woman he had met on one of his tours. My dad, a staunch Catholic, was consumed by guilt and remorse for his actions. The weight of his mistake overwhelmed him. According to my mother, when she first saw him in the hospital, he was so devastated that he couldn't even speak or recognize her.

When my father finally came home, he was a changed man. The quiet, stoic ex-Marine I knew had become much more emotional and talkative. He'd cry over simple things, like a sentimental TV commercial or while telling a story from his past. Physically, he began to deteriorate as well—his hair fell out, he grew a beer belly, and dark circles formed under his eyes from the sleepless nights battling his illness. He was on several powerful medications, but despite his struggles, something remarkable happened: his illness brought us closer than we had ever been before.

Though my father experienced deep periods of sadness due to his depression, he also had moments where his spirit soared with dreams and optimism. He would share these aspirations with me, something he had never done before. With my older brother in the Navy, my father's attention turned to me and my two sisters in those moments of happiness; he even began to express his belief in my singing talent. He suggested that instead of focusing so much on sports, I join him on his bus tours and sing for the tourists.

Inspiring Emcee Dreams

That's when I started accompanying my dad on his tour bus, singing for visitors to Kaua'i. Those rides became special to me. My father wasn't just a great tour guide—he was an incredible storyteller and entertainer. He had a good singing voice and a deep love for Hawaiian history, which he eagerly shared with the tourists. His tours were filled with stories about legendary Hawaiian figures and the rich culture of our island. The first books I ever read cover to cover were the Hawaiian history books he kept at home, which we'd discuss for hours on end.

On his tours, my dad would weave together Hawaiian history, jokes, and heartfelt stories, captivating everyone on the bus. He was a natural entertainer, and the tourists loved him for it. They often filled his pockets with tips as a token of their appreciation for his tours and the island he loved so much. Those experiences on the tour bus deepened my connection with my father and instilled in me a greater appreciation for our culture and heritage.

At the close of most of my father's tours, there was always a final, particular destination: the Coco Palms Hotel. This was no ordinary stop—it was where Larry Rivera dazzled audiences at his legendary luau show and where Elvis filmed scenes for *Blue Hawaii*. My father was well-loved by the managers and staff at the Coco Palms, and they treated me like royalty, offering me a front-row seat to the show and a free meal. Their kindness showed me the true essence of the "Spirit of Aloha."

I spent countless evenings mesmerized by Larry Rivera as he strummed his guitar and sang original Hawaiian songs, his voice captivating the audience. He often spoke about his friendship with Elvis Presley, sharing stories that revealed the superstar's kindness and generosity. Larry would also guide the audience through the iconic scenes from *Blue Hawaii*, many of which were filmed right there at the Coco Palms.

The hotel itself was beautiful—a place with a uniquely Hawaiian flavor in every detail of its design, both inside and out. It was one of the few spots I can remember that truly embraced the essence of the islands. Both Larry and my father made sure everyone knew that the grounds of the Coco Palms were special, steeped in the rich history and culture of the Hawaiian people.

When I returned home with my father after those long days on tour, we would talk about my dreams. I wanted to be like Larry Rivera, writing my own songs and performing at a luau. While I knew that making it as a singer beyond Kaua'i might be a long shot, becoming a performer at a luau seemed like a dream within reach. Those nights at the Coco Palms inspired me, planting a seed that grew and filled me with possibility.

Although my confidence as a singer soared, I couldn't completely step away from the world of sports. I decided to hang up my baseball glove, but my dad, being a great supporter of my singing, didn't make a big deal of it. He knew where my true passion lay. However, there was one sport I couldn't give up—football. There's a thrill in football that's hard to describe, but one of the most exhilarating moments I've ever experienced was running onto the field, pads on, with a stadium full of people cheering us on. There's something about the raw energy of laying it all out on the field. For me, football wasn't just a game but an art form.

Beyond our shared love of history and music, football was another thread that wove my father and me together. Saturdays were reserved for Notre Dame games, and Sundays were all about the 49ers. These were not just games but sacred moments that brought us closer. With my dad not focused so much on my athletics, I was able to turn my attention toward music and began taking guitar lessons at church with my best friends. Yet, Sundays remained special. We'd start the day early, attending Mass together, where I'd play music with my friends, and then we'd spend the rest of the day at the beach, fishing and tossing the football around, all while keeping an ear on the 49ers' game. For us, sports were more than just competition; they were a way to bond, laugh, eat, and share stories as "ohana" or family.

Growing up, my family lived a modest life. I shared earlier how one of the most embarrassing parts of my childhood was lining up for tokens at school each morning. But what *really* made me cringe was the thought of my friends riding in our cars. Most of them were old and rusty, but the one that stands out the most in my memory is a car we affectionately called "The Rambler." Given to us for a dollar by my Aunty Maryanne and Uncle Johnny, The Rambler was an old car, but it was ours. I learned how to drive with that car on the cane field roads of Kaua'i as most young kids did then. My dad loved that car—keeping it running was his little project. He'd tinker with the engine, patch up the rusted chrome bumpers with chrome tape, and even tape the windows together with clear tape. The car had its quirks, like the holes in the floor covered by thick floormats that couldn't entirely block out the smell of gas fumes seeping through. And then there was the color—an unusually light blue resulting from my dad's friends mixing leftover paint from the buses they worked on. The final shade was so unique that my friends dubbed it "Mahu blue," a playful nod to its flamboyant hue.

I'll never forget the day my dad showed up at the end of football practice. We had a deal—he would never drive the Rambler too close to the practice field because, frankly, I didn't want anyone outside our neighborhood to see that the Rambler was our car. My dad respected my wishes and would always park next to the tennis courts, a pleasant minute-long walk from the football field so no one would see it was our automobile. But one day, the rain was pouring, the kind of rain that made some parents think twice about driving out to pick up their kids. As practice ended, a few of my teammates, whose parents were either delayed or discouraged by the weather, asked if they could catch a ride with me and my dad. I tried everything I could to persuade them to get a ride with someone else, but they were persistent, and my dad, proud of the Rambler, was happy to help.

What should have been a quick fifteen-minute ride home turned into an agonizing ordeal that felt like hours. It started the moment my teammates tried to get into the car. Only one of the two back doors worked, but the rain was coming down so hard they couldn't hear me shouting, "Eh, guyz, gotta use da right side fo get in!" They eventually squeezed into the car, drenched and still in their sweaty uniforms. Almost immediately, the windows fogged up, trapping the scent of wet gear, body odor, and the unmistakable fumes that seeped up from the car's floorboards. The smell was, well, let's just say it was not good.

But the fun didn't stop there. A couple of minutes into the ride, one of my friends shouted, "I no can breade! I gotta open da window!" I was about to yell "NO!" but it was too late. My friend in the front passenger seat tried to open the triangular vent window, the one that was barely holding on with tape. Three seconds later, the window flew off, soaring into the air and shattering on the road behind us. All five passengers in the car turned their heads and were in complete shock for about five seconds. Then, they began to laugh hysterically. I braced myself, expecting my dad to be furious, but he just smiled and said calmly, "Don't worry! I can replace it!"

As if that wasn't enough, the cherry on top was when they noticed my dad's creative solution to the broken windshield wipers. He was calmly pulling and releasing a Sugi string attached to the wiper, back and forth, to clear the rain from the windshield so he could see. My friends didn't say a word to my dad, but the story of that ride spread like wildfire. From that day on, the legend of the Rambler was told and retold at every party, a tale of unexpected hilarity, ingenuity, and a father's quiet resilience and humility.

During this stage of my life, I began to explore songwriting while trying to become more proficient at playing the guitar and piano. However, every song I attempted to write during those pre-teen years sounded like a poor imitation of something already out there. Looking back, I realize now that writing music isn't just about creativity; it's also a craft that requires dedication, practice, and a shift in mindset for someone like me. I didn't yet understand the value of reaching out for guidance or instruction at that age, so my songwriting endeavors were mostly trial and error. It wasn't until later in life that I truly began to find my voice as a songwriter. Had I mastered the art of writing music at that age, my life as a recording artist might have taken a very different path.

Thankfully, playing music at St. Raphael Church on Kaua'i every Sunday became my saving grace. Instead of struggling with sheet music, I learned to play songs using chord charts. The Director of Music Ministry at St. Raphael Church introduced me and my friends to the basics of music in a way that made sense to us. He showed us simple patterns on the keyboard and guitar, which made it possible for us to play almost any song we wanted by just notating the chords next to the lyrics. Before this, playing piano and guitar had felt like a chore because reading music demanded a level of discipline I didn't have at the time. But everything clicked once I grasped the fundamental laws and patterns of music. Playing by ear became second nature, and I grew more confident with each note.

Father Felix, who encouraged us to play music during Mass, was instrumental in this phase of my musical journey. Singing each Sunday not only helped me grow as a musician but also deepened my faith in God and strengthened the bonds I shared with my "brothers" from Koloa Elementary School and, later, Kaua'i High School. Even today, I remain close to those friends who became like family to me. They nicknamed me "Pocho Kid" or "Poch" because I was the only non-Filipino in the group, being of pure Portuguese descent. Like the music we played, that nickname became a part of my identity.

This chapter of my life was not just about learning chords and singing hymns but about finding passion, my place in a community, and laying the foundation for the artist I would eventually become. As I look back, I see that these experiences were the seeds that would later blossom into a lifelong passion for music and a deeper appreciation for the friendships and faith that sustained me through those years.

Chapter 4

DISCOVERING THE STAGE

As I moved from childhood into adolescence, my world began to expand beyond the familiar confines of church and family. As mentioned earlier, the first musical I performed in was at my elementary school, where my music teacher had written an original play. I was cast in a singing role, a responsibility that both excited and terrified me. The lights, the audience, the pressure of remembering my lines and hitting the right notes—it was overwhelming but exactly what I needed at the time.

The thrill of that performance was something I'd never forget. Standing in front of my classmates, teachers, and parents, I felt a rush of adrenaline, unlike anything I'd experienced before. When the play ended, and the applause began, it was as if a door had opened to a world I hadn't known existed—a world where my presence on stage could move people.

From that moment on, I sought out every opportunity to perform. Whether it was at school talent shows, community events, or even just impromptu performances with friends, I was drawn to the stage. I relished the chance to sing in front of an audience, to feel the connection that formed when people listened to my voice. It fueled a new kind of confidence in me—one that would carry me through my various stages of life.

As my confidence grew, so did my ambition. I began entering talent contests across Kaua'i, eager to see where these opportunities would take me. The competitions were intense and filled with anticipation. I remember the moments before stepping onto the stage—my heart pounding, my palms sweaty, as I waited for my name to be called. But once I was up there, with the spotlight shining down and the audience watching, everything else faded away. It was just me and the music.

Winning some of those contests felt incredible. Each victory was a validation of the hard work I'd put in, a confirmation that I was on the right path. But more than the trophies or the accolades, what I cherished most was the sense of accomplishment—the feeling that I was moving closer to achieving my dreams.

Yet, not every contest ended in triumph. There were times when I didn't win. Those moments were tough, especially after tasting success. But they were also some of the most valuable lessons I learned. Through those losses, I came to understand the subjectivity of art—that what one person loves, another might not like at all. Beauty is in the eye of the beholder, so to speak. But even when I didn't win, if I could touch just one person in the audience, it was worth it.

Growing up, I spent countless hours listening to love songs by artists like Barry Manilow, Air Supply, and George Benson. Those songs made me believe that the greatest form of happiness is being in a state of love. The irony, though, was that I was too shy to take the initiative to speak with girls. But then I met someone who wasn't shy at all, and she quickly let me know she wanted to get to know me better. Soon after, that person became my first love.

Suddenly, my greatest objective was to find a way to see her as often as possible. That meant getting a car, which in turn meant getting a job. Remembering that

Elvis once worked at a gas station before he became famous, I thought it was a cool place to start.

For the next year and a half, I worked at Chevron in Koloa, and with my hard-earned money, I bought my first car, a small Toyota that my friends affectionately called "Yellow Banana" because of its unique yellow color. It wasn't much, but it gave me the freedom to drive wherever I wanted, especially to my girlfriend's house. That little car became a symbol of my independence, a way to navigate the complexities of teenage love and the responsibilities that came with it.

One of the most memorable moments from that time was coming home after a date, only to find my mother laughing hysterically as I walked into the house.

"So, how did it go, Glenn?"

I tried to keep it casual, telling her about our day at the beach, but she wasn't fooled.

"Is that all you did?" she teased and giggled.

I asked, "Why?"

"Well," she said, "Oh, no reason."

I responded by telling her I had my first, second, third, and fourth kiss. One of the things I've always appreciated about my mother was that I could be open and honest with her. We not only enjoyed singing together, we laughed together quite often.

My first serious relationship taught me a great deal about love, but also about being responsible. My girlfriend's parents, especially her father, played a significant role in this. They welcomed me into their home with open arms, treating me with kindness and respect. Her father, a retired Japanese-American high school typing teacher, was a man of few words, but when he spoke, his advice was always meaningful.

He often talked to me about the importance of saving money and making wise investments—lessons that would stick with me long after the relationship ended. I admired him greatly, not just for his financial wisdom but for the way he loved and cared for his family. He was another role model in my life, someone who embodied the values I hoped to live by—a devoted father, a dedicated teacher, and a man who enjoyed a simple yet fulfilling life in Hawaii.

In many ways, my relationship with my first girlfriend and her family broadened my perspective on life. It showed me that love could exist outside the bounds of family and that people unrelated to me could care deeply for my well-being. Her father's wisdom wasn't just about finances; it was about living a life of integrity and thoughtfulness. His approach to life—simple yet deeply fulfilling—resonated with me, shaping my own aspirations for the future.

Balancing Work, Love, and Music

As I juggled my job at the Chevron station, my relationship, and my passion for music, I often found myself stretched thin. Amidst this whirlwind, another opportunity arose—one that would bring music back to the forefront of my life in a significant way. My former high school band teacher, Larry McIntosh, reached out to me, inviting me to join the high school concert band. The invitation was both surprising and exhilarating. Despite my busy schedule, I couldn't resist the chance to reconnect with music.

Larry McIntosh, or Mr. Mac as we called him, was a legend at Kaua'i High School. His band was the pride of the school, known for its excellence and its ability to bring out the best in every student. Joining the band was a commitment, but it was also an opportunity to learn from one of the best. Under Mr. Mac's guidance,

I quickly realized that music wasn't just about talent—it was about discipline, dedication, and the relentless pursuit of excellence.

Lessons in Excellence

Mr. McIntosh was more than just a band teacher; he was a mentor who saw potential in every student and pushed us to reach it. He had a way of making you believe that you could achieve greatness if you were willing to work for it. His expectations were high, and while he was quick to laugh and joke, he didn't tolerate mediocrity. If you were in his band, you were expected to give your all and nothing less.

One of the most impactful lessons I learned from Mr. McIntosh came during a jazz band rehearsal. He had asked me to play guitar, but the chords were far more complex than anything I had encountered before. Despite hours of practice, I couldn't quite grasp them. Nervously, I approached Mr. Mac, expecting disappointment. Instead, he simply smiled and said, "Don't worry, Glenn. We have two other guitar players, so just go out there and fake it till you make it!"

That night, while we performed at a hotel for a special event, I took his advice to heart. There, I played the best air guitar of my life, and Mr. McIntosh, ever the showman, pointed to me during parts of the song as if I were nailing each note. The experience was both humbling and empowering. It taught me the importance of confidence, even when you're unsure of yourself, and the value of showing up and giving your best, no matter the circumstances.

As I navigated the complexities of love, work, and music, I felt the pieces of my life slowly falling into place. Each experience—whether it was a performance, a relationship, or a lesson learned—was shaping me into the person I was becoming.

The future was wide open, and I was ready to embrace it with all the passion and determination I had. Little did I know that these early experiences—rooted in family, love, and music—would serve as the foundation for a journey that would take me far beyond the shores of my island home. It was the beginning of a new chapter, one filled with endless possibilities, challenges, and dreams waiting to be realized.

Chapter 5

INFLUENCE AND DIRECTION

As I continued to grow both personally and musically, I encountered people who would profoundly shape my life—mentors who saw something in me that I was beginning to recognize in myself. These were not just teachers; they were guides, role models, and, in many ways, the architects of my future.

One of the most influential of these mentors was previously mentioned, Arnold Meister, my elementary music and science teacher. Mr. Meister was a man of immense talent and passion who could transform a group of awkward teenagers and turn them into confident performers. He had a unique ability to see potential where others might find only inexperience. Under his guidance, I began to explore the depths of my creativity, learning to express myself not just through song but through acting as well.

While Mr. Meister nurtured my skills on the stage, Mr. Mac also shaped my musical journey. He was nothing short of a legend, and his reputation as an extraordinary musician and teacher reached every corner of the island. He was another example of a person who chose to teach rather than live in New York or L.A. and become a successful musician. He was not only an incredible saxophone player, but he was also a passionate motivator who taught us that hard work and dedication lead to excellence.

Joining the high school concert band under Mr. Mac's direction was a significant turning point for me. The band was more than just a school activity—it was a symbol of excellence, a place where students could hone their musical talents and push themselves to new heights. Mr. Mac demanded the best from us, and in return, he gave us the tools and guidance we needed to succeed.

From the moment I joined, I felt the intensity of his expectations. Mr. Mac's rehearsals were rigorous, and the pressure was high, but the rewards were immense. Under his leadership, the band consistently won competitions and earned accolades, not just on Kaua'i but across the state. Being part of that group was both an honor and a responsibility, one that I took very seriously.

My time in the concert band was just one part of my high school musical experience. Mr. Mac also led the pep band and jazz band, and he often asked me to participate in these groups as well. The pep band was a high-energy ensemble that performed at football games, rallying the crowd with upbeat tunes and infectious enthusiasm. Playing in the pep band was a different kind of thrill—one that combined the joy of music with the excitement of school spirit.

On the other hand, the jazz band was where I truly began to explore my musical potential. Jazz was a genre that demanded not just technical skill but also creativity. Mr. Mac, being an exceptional saxophonist, had a deep love for jazz, and he was determined to pass that passion on to us.

Traveling with the Concert Band and a New Love

One of the highlights of my high school years was traveling with the concert and jazz bands to perform in competitions and special events. These trips were more than just opportunities to showcase our talents; they were adventures that brought us closer together as a group and deepened our love for music.

During my sophomore year, it was at one of these band trips on the mainland that I met a girl who would become an important part of my life. There was an instant connection between us. Like my previous relationship, this one began with friendship but quickly grew into much more.

Our relationship was different in many ways. We were not only in love but also best friends. We shared a deep connection, one that went beyond the typical teenage romance. We could talk for hours about anything and everything—about our dreams, our fears, our hopes for the future. There was an ease and comfort between us that made our time together feel effortless.

Her family, too, welcomed me with open arms. Like my first girlfriend's family, they were college-educated and placed a high value on education. Her father was Japanese American, and her mother was Portuguese American, just like me. This shared heritage brought us even closer together, and I felt a strong bond with them.

Spending time with her family challenged me to look at life differently, with a new perception, to think about my future in a way I hadn't before. They talked about the importance of education and about the opportunities that a college degree could provide. For them, college wasn't just about getting a job; it was about expanding your horizons, experiencing new things, and growing as a person.

These conversations made me seriously consider college as an option for the first time in my life. My family hadn't emphasized it, but I started to see its value, especially since I had begun to think about becoming a teacher—a goal that was taking shape in my mind.

In my family, college wasn't a goal that anyone really talked about. Our focus was centered more on having faith in God and being good people—values my girlfriend's family shared as well. However, at her home, even the simple activities were more focused on education. We'd play games like Trivial Pursuit and Scrabble or watch movies and discuss the characters and their roles. This kind of critical thinking was relatively new to me. It wasn't that I saw one environment as better than the other; it was just clear that her family placed a strong emphasis on the importance of thinking at a high cognitive level, a particular message I needed to hear, especially as I considered my future as a teacher.

Looking back, I realize how fortunate I was to have had mentors like Mr. Mac and Mr. Meister. They were not just teaching acting and music; they were teaching me the characteristics I needed to be a professional in the music industry—how to strive for excellence, how to work together, and how to face challenges with resilience and grace. Their guidance was a beacon during those formative years, helping me navigate the complexities of adolescence and setting me on a path that would shape my future.

I was no longer the shy kid who had started out singing hymns in church or performing on my father's bus. I had grown into a more confident young man, ready to take on the world with a passion for music and a desire to make a difference. The lessons I had learned from my mentors—Mr. Meister, Mr. Mac, and others—gave me strength for the journey ahead, one that would take me far beyond my island home of Kaua'i.

Chapter 6

DREAMS TAKING SHAPE

Music, which had always been a passion and a way to express myself, was quickly becoming something more—an all-consuming dream I was determined to turn into reality. During this time, I began to seriously consider a career in music, spurred on by the encouragement of those around me and the small successes I had already achieved.

The journey began in earnest when I decided to enter a popular talent contest in Hawaii called "Brown Bags to Stardom." It was a big deal on the islands—a state championship that gave young performers a platform to showcase their talents in front of a large audience. I had participated in the contest during my freshman year, but despite giving it my all, I didn't place in the top three at the state finals. The experience was humbling, yet it fueled my determination to improve and try again the following year.

By the time the next year rolled around, I was ready. Armed with the lessons I had learned from my previous attempt, I poured my heart and soul into my performance. This time, my efforts paid off—I won the Brown Bags to Stardom Championship. The victory was more than just a personal triumph; it was a validation of all the hard work I had put in, a sign that perhaps, just perhaps, my dreams of becoming a professional singer weren't so far-fetched after all.

The prize for winning the Brown Bags to Stardom competition was an opportunity to record a song at no cost. This was my first real introduction to the recording studio. The recording session was set up through KIKI/I-94, a top-rated radio station in Hawaii, and the program director, Jay Stone, took an immediate interest in my potential as an artist.

Jay Stone was more than just a program director; he was a man with aspirations of becoming a music producer, someone who had a keen ear for music that could become a hit. He had a knack for spotting talent and knew how to guide young artists toward success.

When he asked me what song I wanted to record, I hesitated. I had been thinking about choosing an original song that would set me apart, but Jay had other ideas. He suggested I record "Nothing's Gonna Change My Love for You," a song originally recorded by George Benson.

I was hesitant at first. George Benson's version was iconic, and I wasn't sure if I could do it justice. But Jay was persuasive. He pointed out that Whitney Houston had recently covered another Benson song, "The Greatest Love of All," written by the same songwriter, and it had become a massive hit. He believed that with the right timing and promotion, my version of "Nothing's Gonna Change My Love for You" could find similar success.

Reluctantly, I agreed to record the George Benson song I'd sung in the contest. Even though Benson's version was musically superior, sometimes timing is everything. Little did I know this decision would change the course of my life forever.

The recording session was a whirlwind of excitement. I was new to the professional music scene, and the experience of being in a studio surrounded by experienced musicians and sound engineers was both thrilling and intimidating. But as soon as I stepped up to the microphone, all my doubts melted away. I poured everything I had into the performance, determined to make the song my own.

When the session was over, I felt a sense of accomplishment, but I had no idea what the future held. I had done my best, but in the music industry, nothing is guaranteed. Jay Stone, however, was confident. He believed in the song, and he believed in me. He began playing the track on KIKI/I-94, and to our surprise and delight, it quickly became one of the most requested songs on the station.

The response was overwhelming. Listeners loved the song, and it was only a short time before it spread to other radio stations across Hawaii. But the real breakthrough came when Jay sent the track to a friend of his, a program director at a radio station in Phoenix, Arizona. As a favor to Jay, the station began playing the song, and just like in Hawaii, it quickly rose to the top of the request list.

As the song gained momentum, it caught the attention of Lenny Silver, the owner of an independent record label called Amherst Records. Lenny was on vacation in Arizona when he first heard the song on the radio. Intrigued, he contacted the station, discovered that I was not signed to a major label, and immediately reached out to Jay Stone. Before I knew it, I was offered a recording contract with Amherst Records.

The decision to sign with Lenny's independent recording label, Amherst Records, was not an easy one. Lenny Silver became not only my record label owner but also my manager. I knew that signing to an independent record label made it less likely for the song to be as successful as it would have been if the networking and power of a major label were behind it. However, Lenny had a good reputation in the music business as a record distributor, owner of a chain of record stores in New York, and the owner of a recording label. Furthermore, no one else was knocking on my door at the time to work with me.

Once the contract was signed, the real work began. Lenny was determined to make "Nothing's Gonna Change My Love for You" a hit not just in Hawaii but across the United States. He pulled out all the stops, using his connections in the industry to get the song played on as many radio stations as possible. The response was positive, but the real breakthrough came when Lenny reached out to his friend Doc

Severinsen, a famous jazz musician and the leader of *The Tonight Show's* band. Lenny managed to secure me a spot on one of the most popular television shows of the time with Johnny Carson!

The invitation to perform on *The Tonight Show* was a dream come true. For any artist, appearing on Johnny Carson's show was a mark of success, a chance to reach millions of viewers across the country. I was both thrilled and terrified at the prospect.

When I arrived in Los Angeles for the show, I was introduced to Doc Severinsen. Doc was signed to Amherst Records as well, and it was through his connection with Lenny that I had been given this incredible opportunity. Doc suggested that I perform the song live with the band rather than with a pre-recorded track. The idea was daunting—this was *The Tonight Show* Band, after all—but I knew it was the right choice.

The day of the performance was a blur of rehearsals, sound checks, and last-minute nerves. As I stood backstage in the "green room," waiting for my cue, I could feel my heart pounding in my chest. Millions of people would be watching—this was the biggest moment of my career so far. Right before performing, Doc told me that if Johnny liked my singing, he would invite me to speak with him on the couch next to him. I just assumed that he would not, so I didn't prepare to speak with him.

The performance went off without a hitch, and when I finished the song, the audience gave me a standing ovation. To my surprise and delight, Johnny Carson himself waved me over to the famous couch. Sitting there, talking with Johnny, was surreal. He was gracious and kind, making me feel at ease despite the overwhelming situation. Johnny also thought it was hilarious that I was from Hawaii and my manager was from Buffalo, New York.

When we went to break, Johnny made it a point to thank me personally for the gift from the Mayor of Kaua'i and my good friend who worked for him, Art Umezu. It was a large Koa bowl filled with local products—which he loved and appreciated. He said he had never received such a lovely gift in all his years.

The Impact of The Tonight Show

My appearance on *The Tonight Show* was the catalyst that propelled "Nothing's Gonna Change My Love for

You" into the spotlight. Almost overnight, the song started climbing the charts, gaining airplay not just on the West Coast but nationwide. It eventually reached number 12 on the Billboard Top 40 chart—a remarkable feat for a relatively unknown artist from Hawaii.

To help promote the song, Lenny asked me if I wanted to record a music video. I loved the idea and shared that I wanted to record it on the island of Kaua'i, at several of my favorite beaches. I encouraged many of my high school friends to audition for the video, but in the end, the person they chose to be my love interest in the video was someone I had never met before. Filming the video was a surreal experience—we held hands, ran on the beach, and were even asked to kiss. It was strange kissing someone I didn't know, but the best part was that we didn't take ourselves too seriously and had fun with it. Looking back, I think my first music video was the best one I ever did. Everything about it felt natural—it was filmed at home, featured a great song, and matched my style and personality perfectly. That wasn't always the case for much of the other music I eventually made in my career.

The success of the song opened doors I had never imagined. Suddenly, I was invited to perform at major events, appear on other TV shows, and travel across the country to promote the single. It was an exhilarating whirlwind but also incredibly demanding. I was still just a teenager, trying to balance the pressures of a rising music career with the desire to live a normal life.

At the time, Lenny asked if I could move to L.A. or New York to speed up my career as a singer. But I loved my home and the people I was close to and could not make that sacrifice at such a young age. Instead, I decided to stay on Kaua'i for short periods and then head out on the road for a few weeks at a time. I also didn't want to miss out on my high school experience, so I tried to juggle attending school with working as a recording artist and performer.

While the success of "Nothing's Gonna Change My Love for You" was a dream come true, it also came with its own set of challenges. The demands of promoting the song were intense. I found myself constantly on the road, flying from city to city, doing interviews, performing at radio-sponsored events, and trying to win over new fans. The pace was exhausting, and the pressure to maintain the momentum was overwhelming at times. There were days when I would fly back to Kaua'i just to attend school, only to leave again for another promotional tour. The constant travel took its toll, both physically and emotionally. I missed my family, my friends, and the simple pleasures of home. I missed being a normal teenager.

Looking back, the decision to stay on Kaua'i probably hurt my chances of becoming more successful in the U.S. and beyond. Still, thanks to my performance on *The Tonight Show,* my music video became very popular on MTV and led to many more opportunities for me as a professional singer.

Years later, I realized that if I had moved to Los Angeles, my music career could have taken a different path. This thought comes from the fact that "Nothing's Gonna Change My Love for You" eventually achieved number-one status in most of the countries where it was released after being picked up by Polygram Records.

Looking Ahead

As "Nothing's Gonna Change My Love for You" continued to spread in popularity, I began to realize that my life was changing in ways I hadn't anticipated. The dream of becoming a professional singer was no longer just a fantasy—it was becoming a reality. But with that reality came new challenges, new responsibilities, and new decisions that would shape the course of my career.

I knew that the journey ahead would be difficult, that there would be sacrifices to make and obstacles to overcome. But I also knew that I was ready. The experiences I had gone through—the early performances, the talent contests, the mentorships, and now the success of my first major single—had prepared me for this moment. I was ready to embrace the opportunities that lay ahead and continue pursuing my dreams with all the passion and dedication I had.

Chapter 7

THE INTERNATIONAL STAGE

With the success of my first single in the United States, my life was on a fast track I could have never anticipated. The song's rise on the Billboard charts opened up doors not just at home but across the globe. The music industry was beginning to take notice, and suddenly, I found myself being introduced to a world far beyond the shores of Hawaii.

My manager, Lenny Silver, had done an incredible job of promoting the song in the U.S., but he knew that to truly capitalize on its success, we needed to take it international. That's where Polygram Records came into the picture. Polygram was one of the largest record labels in the world, with a vast network that spanned across Europe and Asia. They saw the potential in

"Nothing's Gonna Change My Love for You" and were eager to release it worldwide. Soon after signing with Polygram Records internationally, I also signed with MCA Records in the United States. Signing with both major labels was a monumental step in my career. It meant that I would be venturing into new markets, reaching audiences who had never heard of me before.

Throughout these changes, Lenny Silver continued as my manager. Because he ran several other companies, Lenny had his son Larry represent me whenever I went on tour. Larry was closer to my age and made the experience on the road enjoyable. During those years on the road, we became like brothers.

From the age of sixteen to twenty-two, I journeyed through around thirty countries on tour. Most of this time was spent promoting—doing interviews and performing in small venues or on TV. Larry and I tried to make the most of it, but life on the road was anything but easy. With a tight budget, I couldn't afford to stay in touch with loved ones as often as I wanted, and the hectic schedule, combined with my dislike for flying, made things even tougher.

While traveling the world was tough, I had the opportunity to meet so many fascinating and highly successful individuals who opened my mind in ways that no classroom ever could. It became clear to me that perspective shapes everything—how we think, how we act, and ultimately, how we succeed. The successful people I encountered all seemed to follow a set of unwritten rules. They worked relentlessly, stayed ahead of the curve with the latest technologies, and often had multiple ventures in motion at once, confident that at least one or two would yield substantial returns.

What struck me most wasn't that these people were fundamentally different from me. Instead, they viewed the world through a lens of opportunity and possibility instead of fear. They refused to engage in negativity, choosing instead to focus on sharing ideas and envisioning what could be. Networking was a cornerstone of their success, as was the constant pursuit of "win-win" situations. For them, nothing was impossible.

But perhaps the most powerful lesson I learned from these individuals was their fearless approach to failure. They didn't shy away from mistakes; they embraced them as stepping stones on the path to success. It was their courage and resilience that set them apart.

The European Tour

At eighteen, my career as an artist in Europe seemed to have reached its peak. My song "Nothing's Gonna Change My Love for You" skyrocketed to number one in Scandinavia, capturing the hearts of fans in Norway, Sweden, Finland, and Denmark. With those initial successes, Polygram Records began investing in promoting my music across other countries in Europe.

Soon, my single topped the charts in countries like France, Spain, England, Holland, Belgium, Portugal, Switzerland, and beyond. While I saw modest success in Germany and Italy, the bulk of my European and Asian success came from other regions.

France ranked at the top of the list, and a new opportunity arose unexpectedly. At a time when I often felt isolated, craving the simplicity of just being a kid, I met a French singer, Elsa, and things changed. Elsa was also a teenager and a successful actor and recording artist in France. We first connected on a popular television show after she mentioned in an interview that she enjoyed my music. The producers thought it would be fun to surprise her by having me sing one of her songs from behind a curtain. When I revealed myself, I was then asked to perform "Nothing's Gonna Change My Love For You" for her. I had never heard of Elsa before that moment, and I had no idea what to expect—what she looked like, whether she spoke English. But the moment we met on stage, there was an undeniable connection. She spoke enough English for us to communicate, and we quickly became good friends during that promotional trip.

After the show aired, it received high ratings, and record executives decided it would be a great idea for us to record a duet. We recorded "Love Always Finds a Reason," penned by Diane Warren and Robbie Buchanan, as well as a French version, "My Friend, You Give Me a Reason." Promoting the song took us on a whirlwind tour, and although we were just friends, our bond deepened. I could sense that Elsa's father did not want us to get too close, while her mother did everything she could to allow Elsa to enjoy being a teenager with me. Elsa was very mature for her age, spending most of her time with people much older than her. But when we were together, she could relax, laugh, and just be a kid. It was a relief to have someone my age to share the road with.

However, the constant traveling began to wear on me emotionally. I missed home, my family, and the simple pleasures of life in Hawaii. My time with Elsa felt almost like a dream, filled with unforgettable moments in France, Tahiti, England, and Los Angeles. We shared playful adventures, like chasing each other through the Louvre in Paris and exploring Hyde Park in London. Elsa and I became close, but we both understood that a relationship with someone living on the other side of the world wasn't realistic.

Eventually, our paths diverged. My record company decided I should re-record the song I sang with Elsa and another artist in Holland. In retrospect, I should have told the label that I would not sing the song with anyone else. One of my regrets in my music career was that I often let others make significant decisions for me because I lacked confidence in my own judgment.

Something beautiful came from my time with Elsa, and it inspired me to start writing music. At first, I believed that songwriting was something done naturally. However, I eventually learned it's a craft that requires inspiration and practice. Thanks to guidance from one of my producers, Jeff Tyzik, I began to understand the process of songwriting. Once I had a system in place and let inspiration guide me, the songs began to flow. They were simple, but they fit my voice and style perfectly. Writing my own music not only allowed me to express myself but also provided a significant source of income, something I would explore further in my musical career.

A Fun-Filled Time in Spain

One of the most memorable experiences from this stage of my life was a live tour I did in Spain. I share this because it was one of the most amazing experiences I had as an artist. Beyond the performances, I had an incredible time touring with the band, and I certainly learned a lot along the way. What also made it special was that I brought with me from Hawaii my good friend and musician, Lester Gantan, to play keyboard on tour and lead the band. We had a great time together on tour. Spain was a country where my records had sold exceptionally well—my second album even achieved double platinum status there. This success led a promoter to offer me a live tour across about ten cities. At that point, I had never done a nationwide live tour before. My previous tours were mainly promotional, where I'd sing two or three songs before other successful or up-and-coming artists took the stage. I never enjoyed singing to pre-recorded instrumentals because people often assumed I was lip-syncing, even though I rarely did. I only resorted to it when I was too sick to perform live or when the sound system wasn't set up for a live show. This tour in Spain was my chance to finally live my dream—performing in front of large audiences of around 5,000 to 10,000 people instead of small clubs with 100 to 1,000 often distracted people.

When we arrived in Spain, I think the band was surprised by the number of fans waiting at the airport. While I had some success in the United States, I was far more popular in certain parts of Europe, including Spain. It was amusing to watch my bandmates react to the crowds. At that moment, I knew this tour was going to be something special.

Our journey began with a large, air-conditioned bus waiting for us at the airport. The driver, José, welcomed us aboard. He didn't speak English, but his warm demeanor was enough to make us feel at ease. I remember José being relatively short, so much so that he had to lean forward to reach the oversized steering wheel. We had an interpreter provided by the tour promoter, and she sat at the front, using a microphone to give us instructions. It felt like we were on a school field trip. As we made our way to the first hotel, the interpreter informed us that our concerts would take place in bullrings in the larger cities, seating between 5,000 and 10,000 people. In smaller towns, we'd perform for about 2,000 to 3,000 people on festival stages. She also warned us that most of the bus rides would last between five to ten hours. Once the announcements were over, José hit the gas, and we got our first taste of his driving. Let's just say that José had only one speed—extremely fast. The band members in the back started feeling queasy from the motion but laughed it off.

One of the first concerts we did was for a crowd of about 10,000 people. I'll never forget the roar of the audience that night—it's what every artist dreams of. When I sang "Nothing's Gonna Change My Love for You" at the end of the concert, the entire crowd, as far as I could see, held up lighters and waved them to the rhythm of the song. It was a moment I'll always cherish, as it felt like all my hard work had led to this point. After the concert, security advised me not to enter the bus with the band, but I insisted on joining them. A decoy was sent in a black Mercedes limousine to create a diversion, but the crowd soon realized I was on the tour bus. Waving to fans from my window seat only added to the frenzy. There was a chain-link fence in front of the bus, and I watched as fans tried to climb it all at once. Suddenly, the entire fence collapsed, and a man hurled what looked like a rock directly at me. Fortunately, he missed me by about a foot, but the rock hit the window, causing it to shake violently before shattering. Everyone on the bus hit the floor as the windows continued to rattle. After what felt like an eternity, the shattering stopped, and José sped away to the hotel. That incident was a wake-up call—I never took security lightly after that.

The next morning, José replaced the shattered window with a makeshift plastic cover and tape. The bus looked odd, but the show had to go on. As we approached another town a few days later, one of the band members pointed out something unusual in the distance. It looked like people were running back and forth, and as we got closer, we realized they were chasing a bull. We couldn't help but laugh until our drummer shouted, "The bull is coming for the bus!" Incredibly, the bull was charging at us, and José began driving in circles to avoid it. Despite his efforts, the bull was far more agile than our bus. Suddenly, we heard the screeching sound of metal, followed by our guitarist's voice, "Oh my God, the bull is ripping into the bus!" After what seemed like an eternity, the bull finally ran off, leaving two long scrapes indented on the side of the bus. We couldn't help but laugh at the absurdity of it all, but the tour wasn't over yet.

Toward the end of our tour, the interpreter stood up in the front of the bus to address us. José was flying through the mountains at about 100 miles per hour, and we all knew how dangerous it was for her to stand while the bus was moving at such high speeds. None of us wanted to upset José, who was still shaken from the previous incidents, but our worst fears were realized when José suddenly hit the brakes. The interpreter was flung backward, crashing into the large picture window at the front of the bus. José stopped immediately, and we rushed to help her. Fortunately, she hadn't lost consciousness, but the incident left us all shaken. When we reached the next stop, we saw a huge sunburst-shaped crack in the window where her head had hit. José was in shock.

Before the tour ended, we flew to Mallorca for another concert. Larry and I spent the day riding mopeds across the island while the rest of the band visited the beach. Though our scooters kept breaking down, we made it back safely, having had an adventurous day. Meanwhile, the band members had their own story to tell—unbeknownst to them, the beach they visited was a nude beach. Some of them joined in, while others opted out. The funniest part was hearing about our drummer, who wore nothing but his backstage pass. He wore it everywhere he went to help make new friends. We spent most of the trip mocking him for wearing that backstage pass and nothing else on the beach, but he enjoyed being made fun of because of it.

Traveling the world gave me the chance to witness incredible cathedrals, temples, museums, and natural wonders, all while being guided by locals who knew the best spots. The candid conversations I had with people working at the record labels opened my eyes to different perspectives on America and Americans. Their views challenged me to rethink America's role in the world. At the same time, my travels deepened my appreciation for my country and the many wonderful aspects of living in America.

The Toll of Touring and the Impact of Family

While the European tour was a thrilling adventure, it was also incredibly taxing. The constant travel, the long hours, and the pressure to deliver performances every night began to take a toll on me. Physically, I was exhausted, but emotionally, I was drained as well. Being on the road meant being away from home, away from the people I loved, and that was something I struggled with deeply.

My visits home became my sanctuary—essential for keeping myself grounded amidst the chaos. The relentless cycle of visiting radio stations, convincing them to play my music, and hopping from one city to another each day was exhausting. I often found myself in unfamiliar places, knowing no one but my manager, running on minimal sleep. My days blurred together—morning interviews, brief midday naps, dinners, and performances at radio-sponsored events in exchange for airtime. And then, just a few hours of sleep before it all started again in a new city.

The late 80s were different times. Contacting my loved ones was costly; calling home was a rare luxury, and sending postcards became the most affordable way to stay connected. Flying was another challenge, especially on the small planes we frequently used. The stress of constantly being on the road weighed heavily on me, but returning home to the most beautiful place in the world, to the people I cherished, was my saving grace. It was in these moments that I could truly recover.

When I did make it back home, my time was shared with the people I loved. In particular, the moments I shared with my father were priceless. Each morning, he would visit me on his way to work, and we'd enjoy breakfast together. On days when I couldn't meet him, he would leave breakfast outside my door as a surprise. These small gestures meant the world to me. Needless to say, our bond was incredibly strong.

There were moments when I would reflect on my time on the road and whether this was the life I truly wanted. The fame, the travel, the adoration of fans—it was everything I had dreamed of, but it also came at a cost. The constant pressure to maintain success and to keep up with the demands of the industry was overwhelming at times. I found myself longing for the more simple life I had growing up on Kaua'i.

Chapter 8

LEARNING FROM THE PROS

Over the years, I had the privilege of spending time in the studio with some of the world's most accomplished musicians. Lenny, my manager, ensured we worked with the best talent in the world at the time. From Robbie Buchanan on keyboards to Nathan East on bass, Paul Jackson Jr. and Steve Lukather on guitar, and Jim Robinson on drums, I was fortunate to share the room with some of L.A.'s finest—triple-scale musicians, whose skills were so revered that they earned three times the standard union rate. These artists were masters of their craft, able to hear a song once and deliver an impeccable performance with just one or two takes. For them, pop music was second nature. During breaks, they often jammed together, playing very complicated jazz tunes.

What made these recording sessions truly special was not just the music but the camaraderie. Despite their success—owning multi-million-dollar homes in L.A. complete with their own studios and driving expensive cars—these musicians were incredibly down-to-earth. They shared stories of working with some of my favorite artists, and I learned a great deal just by listening. The producers and writers I collaborated with included legends like Michael Masser, David Foster, Humberto Gatica, Diane Warren, Ray Parker Jr., and members of the band Toto. Each brought their unique touch to the music, and their humility and friendliness made the experience all the more memorable.

On the road, I had the chance to meet many artists I had grown up admiring. Some I worked closely with, while others I only met briefly, but each encounter left its mark. Early in my career, Radio personality Rick Dees thought setting me up on a dinner date with Debbie Gibson would be fun. We were both teenagers experiencing success around the same time, so it made sense. He treated us to one of the best steakhouses in Los Angeles. Debbie's mother and my manager joined us, and after a fantastic meal, Debbie and I spent the night singing *Grease* songs on the balcony of my hotel room in L.A., playing the roles of Danny and Sandy. Debbie was the first person to talk to me about the importance of writing my own music, something I had only been experimenting with at the time.

Touring also meant sharing the stage with groups like New Kids on the Block, Tiffany, Bell Biv DeVoe, The Bangles, Vanilla Ice, The Nelson Brothers, Donny Osmond, Dionne Warwick, Roy Orbison, Tom Jones, Bobby Brown, Natalie Cole, The Jets, and many more. I was a huge fan of The Jets' lead singer and was thrilled to work with her on a song for *The Karate Kid III*. I even made a brief appearance in the movie, sharing a scene with the major actors for about three seconds before a bar fight ensued. The choreographer for the movie was Paula Abdul, and we got to know each other well during the production. I remember giving her some advice about the music industry, and six months later, she became one of the world's most successful artists. It just goes to show—you never know who will make it in this industry. Paula had the talent, but so did many others I had similar conversations with who didn't reach the same heights.

Of all the celebrities I met, each left a particularly strong impression on me—Magic Johnson, Prince,

Huey Lewis, Johnny Carson, Elton John, Ray Parker Jr., David Foster, Natalie Cole, Rick James, Bobby Brown, and Joan Rivers were amazing, and some I got to know better than others. Magic Johnson, in particular, had a way of filling the room with positivity. When he met me, he knew my background and the songs I performed, and he treated me like a genuine fan. I later realized that this was his gift—making everyone around him feel important and valued. Prince, on the other hand, was quiet and reserved. Meeting him in his studio and watching him play basketball was surreal—I never imagined Prince as someone who enjoyed Doritos, watching TV, and shooting hoops. It was a reminder that no matter how someone appears in public, there's always more to their personality.

Huey Lewis was one of the most down-to-earth people I ever met. We crossed paths in England on a television show and again at a 49ers game in the VIP box. Like me, he is a huge 49ers fan. I also had the chance to attend Babyface's birthday party, where I found myself seated across from Elton John. Despite his fame, Elton was kind and approachable, and Ray Parker Jr. was the epitome of cool. He could play any instrument, write hit songs effortlessly, and even pilot a plane. Despite my fear of flying in small aircrafts, he convinced me to join him for a ride one night during a recording session. Ray was just that charismatic.

David Foster once invited me to his home in California. We spent hours discussing his iconic songs, and he even played a few of them on the piano while I sang along. At the end of our time together, he showed me a video of a young girl from Canada he was eager to work with and asked if I would be interested in singing with her. I was intrigued, but for some reason, the opportunity never materialized. That young girl turned out to be Celine Dion, who soon became a global superstar.

Then there was Rick James, whom I met through my manager, Lenny, who also lived in Buffalo, New York. Rick was laid-back, intelligent, and incredibly cool. During our visit, I mentioned that I was looking for someone to rap on a hip-hop track I was working on. Without missing a beat, Rick called up Bobby Brown and asked if he'd collaborate with me. It was surreal—this was at the height of Bobby's career, yet he immediately agreed to work with me. Working with Bobby Brown was eye-opening. Despite his immense talent and success, like many other successful artists, he struggled with addiction, a battle he was brave enough to speak about publicly. I admire Bobby for sharing his story to help others avoid the same pitfalls. In his prime, Bobby was arguably the most talented singer and performer I've ever worked with.

One of my most unforgettable encounters was with Joan Rivers. Before interviewing me on her show, she asked to speak with me privately. Knowing I was still a teenager, Joan wanted to offer some advice. She warned me against plastic surgery, saying some doctors could ruin my face as she felt they had done to hers. She also cautioned me never to give anyone power of attorney, a mistake she had seen others make. Despite her busy schedule, Joan took the time to offer me this wisdom, showing that she cared about my well-being. She was a beautiful person, inside and out, and I'll always be grateful for that small moment in time that she took away from her personal schedule to give me some advice.

Reflecting on these experiences, I realize how fortunate I was to have crossed paths with so many incredibly talented and influential people. From recording in studios with some of the world's best musicians to sharing stages with iconic artists, every moment added a layer to my understanding of the industry and of myself. Each encounter, whether it was a late-night jam session or a casual dinner, left an indelible mark on my journey. The lessons I learned—from the importance of humility and hard work to the value of connecting with others—shaped not just my career but also my character. As I navigated the highs and lows of fame, these interactions served as reminders of what truly matters: the relationships we build, the stories we share, and the growth that comes from every experience, whether it be joyful or challenging. As I move forward, these memories remain a source of inspiration, guiding me as I continue to create, connect, and evolve both as an artist and as a person.

Chapter 9

BIG TRANSITIONS

After experiencing success as a pop/ballad singer in Europe in the late 1980s, it was time to begin working on a new record in Los Angeles in 1990 with MCA Records. Before starting, I met with the record executives to share my vision for continuing to sing ballads and soft pop-rock—the style that had brought me success and connected with my audience. I was confident this was the right path to sustain my career. However, executives immediately rejected the idea. The Artist and Repertoire executive at MCA Records told me that if I wanted to pursue that style of music, I would have to find a new record deal. The bluntness of that statement hit me hard. I was devastated by the response, especially since I had just purchased a home on Kaua'i and had a mortgage to pay. Although I had made a reasonable amount of money in the music business, I wasn't in a financial position to walk away from my record deal and wait for another company to potentially sign me.

The truth is, like many entertainers who sold thousands of records, touring was challenging and expensive. Most artists barely break even on tour after covering costs for band members, travel, and other expenses—especially those with just one hit record. The lifestyle that fans often envision—luxurious and carefree—is far from the reality for many artists. Additionally, copyright laws in the United States favor writers, guaranteeing them income with every record sold. Had I written my music in the early years of my career, even with one hit, I would have made significantly more money and been in a stronger position to negotiate. Instead, I was given an ultimatum: if I wanted to keep my record deal, I would have to record a hip-hop album, as that was the trend then. It was a stark reminder of how little control artists can have over their careers, especially when they don't hold the rights to their music.

I must admit, I enjoyed listening to hip-hop music. Growing up, I sang a lot of R&B because many of my favorite artists were singers like George Benson, Michael Jackson, James Ingram, Jeffrey Osborne, Marvin Gaye, and others. These artists profoundly impacted me, and their music deeply influenced how I approached singing. However, I couldn't imagine myself performing hip-hop on stage. My rhythm was decent, but I wasn't a dancer, and the idea of performing hip-hop didn't align with who I was as an artist. MCA Records had reasons for wanting me to make the shift. In 1990, the music industry was moving steadily away from pop songs to grunge and hip-hop, and pop singers like myself were becoming less popular. The industry was in flux, and labels scrambled to stay relevant by aligning their artists with the latest trends. What I didn't consider deeply enough was how this change would affect my fans and the message it would send. I had built my career on a particular style, a certain sound, and to suddenly pivot to something so different felt like a betrayal of myself and my audience.

I could have taken a stand, as Prince did, and shopped my ideas around until I found a label willing to let me create the music I wanted. Prince had always been an icon of artistic integrity, refusing to compromise his vision for the sake of commercial success. I admired his courage to stand firm in his artistic convictions. But I had also heard of too many artists who took that route and ended up without a new recording deal, their careers stalling or fading entirely. In this case, I chose to take the safer path and follow MCA Records' direction, hoping to make the best of the situation and perhaps even find a way to infuse some of my style into the hip-hop sound they wanted.

One of the harsh realities of the music industry is that talent alone doesn't always lead to fame and success. Networking is a crucial part of an artist's journey. The relationships you build and the connections you form can be just as influential to your success as your talent and abilities. Unfortunately, networking meant more than just professional relationships; in many cases, I saw others entering into personal relationships with executives, managers, or others to advance their careers.

In some cases, the relationships created were casual and friendly for both parties, but there were definitely more serious relationships intertwined, creating powerful alliances that propelled careers forward. I also witnessed situations where older, more powerful individuals tried to take advantage of young people like myself, offering fame in exchange for intimacy. These were dark undercurrents in an industry that often portrayed itself as glamorous and exciting.

Fortunately, I never gave in to those temptations, but my mistake was not being true to myself as an artist and allowing others to make decisions for me that I knew weren't in my best interest. The pressure to conform, to please the label, and to ensure financial stability led me to choices that, in hindsight, were not aligned with my true artistic identity.

The music industry can be brutal, with its peaks and valleys. Some artists managed to withstand the financial ups and downs because they were independently wealthy before entering the business, allowing them to be patient and selective about their choices. They had the luxury of waiting out the lean times, of saying no to projects that didn't align with their vision. Others turned to alternative forms of income, like selling drugs, to make ends meet on the road. It was a dangerous path, but for some, it was the only way to survive the unpredictability of a career in music. I also saw artists who were practically owned by their managers, stripped of everything they once had, including their homes and cars. These managers used their leverage to force artists into unfair contracts or deals, controlling their lives to the point where they had little say in their careers or finances. I learned early on that if someone offers to take care of everything for you, it's often a trap. Fortunately, I didn't fall for that, but looking back, I can see that choosing to record a hip-hop album was not the best decision for my career in the long term. It was a decision made out of fear, out of a desire to please others rather than staying true to myself.

Nonetheless, it was time to start working on my new R&B record with MCA Records. They brought in two talented R&B/pop songwriters to work with me. One was an excellent keyboardist who had just finished working with Quincy Jones, a legend in the industry whose influence on music was unparalleled. The other was a successful songwriter with a bright future in Los Angeles, known for her ability to craft catchy, memorable melodies. We began writing songs together in L.A., some of which were entirely new creations, while others were adaptations of their previous work. The process was both exhilarating and challenging. One of the songs we wrote together eventually reached number one on the Billboard charts—"She Ain't Worth It." Although my contribution to the writing was limited to the music itself, I worked closely with the writers, meeting daily to refine the song. I was learning, absorbing their techniques, and trying to find a way to make this music feel like it was mine, even though it wasn't entirely in my comfort zone. When the song was recorded, it sounded like a hit, so we decided to add a rap section. Since Bobby Brown and I were both signed to MCA and he was between records, the label thought it would be a good idea to feature him as the rapper on the track. Bobby was a huge star at the time, and his involvement in the song was seen as a guaranteed way to boost its success.

When Bobby wrote the rap lyrics, he understandably requested a share of the song's ownership as a writer. However, the two writers I had collaborated with were unwilling to give up any of their shares. Instead, they approached me and stated that I hadn't contributed enough to deserve a portion. It was a frustrating situation, but one that could have been avoided if we had signed an agreement before starting, stating that I would receive a portion of the writing credit for any songs we worked on together. This experience taught me an important lesson about the business side of music—one that I wish I had learned earlier. As soon as they knew Bobby was on the record, they realized it would be a hit, and with the full backing of the label, they were determined to protect their interests. I was disappointed, but I continued collaborating with them on the rest of the record, determined to make the best of the situation and learn as much as I could from the process. These types of scenarios often occur in the music industry, and I do not hold anything personally against those involved. I fault myself for not entering into the proper agreement before writing songs with people I had never worked with.

I followed up recording "She Ain't Worth It" with another original song, this time with Bobby as the writer and producer of a hip-hop track called "Lovely Little Lady." Bobby was at the peak of his career and traveled with a large entourage wherever he went. The entourage was part of the package, all of them part of the whirlwind that surrounded him. Unfortunately, it was clear that Bobby was dealing with some of the darker aspects of fame. The pressure, the constant attention, and the demands of being in the spotlight were taking their toll. Some days, he would arrive at the studio in a serious, somber mood, avoiding interaction with most of us. On other days, he was friendly and outgoing, the life of the party, laughing and joking as if nothing was wrong. It was a stark contrast, and it was hard not to feel concerned for him. The life of an entertainer, especially a very successful one, seems glamorous from the outside, but it comes with significant challenges. The highs are incredibly high, but the lows can be devastating. Despite everything, when people ask me about Bobby, I can confidently say that he is a genuinely kind person. Fame and fortune didn't change who he was at his core—a loving father, a loyal friend, and a person who, like all of us, had his struggles.

I can still remember talking to Bobby while we were filming the music video for "She Ain't Worth It." He spoke about his love for his children and his desire to become a billionaire to provide for them for the rest of their lives. He even joked that his record sales would spike each time he was arrested. It's easy to judge people's actions from the outside, but we often don't understand their motivations. People make decisions for various reasons, and it's important not to make assumptions without having walked in their shoes. Bobby's comments were a reminder that the public image of a celebrity is often just that—an image carefully curated and managed, sometimes hiding the true person behind it.

When my hip-hop album was released, MCA made "She Ain't Worth It" their priority. With its catchy tune and Bobby Brown's star power, the song quickly shot up the charts, becoming my first and only number-one hit on the Billboard Top 40 in the United States. The success of the song was exhilarating, but it also felt a bit surreal. This wasn't the music I had envisioned making when I started my career, but here it was, topping the charts. MCA hired two dancers to work with me on choreographed routines for the song, and while they did their best to support my limited dance skills, I could sense that my transition to hip-hop didn't fully convince the audience. I wasn't a dancer, and despite the best efforts of everyone involved, it showed. Although the song was successful in the U.S., it received mixed reviews in Europe and parts of Asia, where many viewed it as a sellout. Looking back, I understand why they felt that way—I had chosen to record a hip-hop album, knowing it didn't reflect who I was as an artist. I was stepping into a role that didn't fit me, and the dissonance was apparent to anyone who knew my earlier work. By the time I realized that my next record needed to be more authentic, the window of opportunity was already closing. I had strayed too far from my roots, and it was going to be a challenge to find my way back.

At twenty-one, I flew to Connecticut to immerse myself in writing a new album filled with original songs that genuinely represented me. This time, I wanted to make music that reflected my true self, music that came from the heart rather than from a place of obligation or external pressure. Unfortunately, by the time it was released, it was too late. The press had already formed their opinions, and my moment to make a successful comeback was slipping away. It was a tough lesson to learn—one about timing, about staying true to oneself, and about the often unforgiving nature of the music industry.

Part of the reason for this was the changing landscape of the music industry. The press in the late 1980s and early 1990s could be supportive at times, but they could also be highly critical, often with little regard for the impact their words had on young artists. I remember one journalist questioning why the world needed another Barry Manilow—a sentiment that reflected the prevailing view that artists like Manilow were corny and outdated. It was a harsh critique, especially since I had always admired Manilow's ability to craft songs that touched people's hearts. But in the eyes of some, his music was seen as too sentimental, too safe. Journalists, especially those who were former musicians, often saw young pop stars as lucky, untalented, and lacking in depth. They viewed us as products of the industry rather than as genuine artists. While there may be some truth to those stereotypes, it's important to remember that teenage artists are still developing their sound and identity. They're at a stage in life where they crave acceptance and love, and their music is often a reflection of their growth.

Teenagers, like anyone else, need time to develop their unique voice. Even the greatest artists go through phases of imitation before finding their own style. Rick James once told me that Prince, who was the opening act at some of his concerts, emulated his style in the early years, and it took time for him to develop the distinctive sound that made him a legend. Prince, like all artists, had to go through a period of exploration, of trying on different musical identities before settling on the one that felt right. There are countless examples of young artists who eventually became superstars, like Michael Jackson and Stevie Wonder. Both Jackson and Wonder started their careers as child stars, but it wasn't until they grew older and gained more control over their music that they truly found their voices. But for most teenage artists, the pressures of the industry and the harsh judgments of the press prove too much to overcome. Some are dismissed as "one-hit wonders," while others struggle to escape the image associated with their early fame.

When people ask me today how it feels to be a "one-hit wonder," I correct them—I'm a two-hit wonder in the U.S. and Asia and a three-hit wonder in Europe. The reality is that many teenage pop stars never recover once their careers fade. Some turn to drugs, while others move on to successful careers in other fields. The transition from fame to obscurity can be a difficult one, and not everyone navigates it successfully. As my singing career began to slow down, I knew I wanted to be in the latter category. I tried to find a way to take the lessons I learned and the experiences I gained to build a fulfilling life, even if it wasn't in the spotlight. The journey wasn't always easy, but it was one that ultimately prepared me for that next stage.

Chapter 10

BACK TO MY ROOTS

After purchasing my home on Kaua'i as a teenager, I never had the chance to live in it for an extended period. My life was a whirlwind of recording sessions, tours, and constant travel, and the island home I had dreamed of felt more like a distant oasis than a place I could actually enjoy. However, as executives at record companies began telling me that my time as a singer had passed, I realized I needed to take a step back. For the first time since I began my professional singing career, I felt an overwhelming need to spend more time with my family and friends at home on Kaua'i while also wanting to develop my skills as a songwriter and arranger.

Those two years, from age twenty-two to twenty-four, became one of the best periods of my life because

I finally took the time to sit back and enjoy my home, friends, and family without the relentless pressure of being on the road. It was as if I was rediscovering life's simple pleasures—playing golf and tennis daily with my father, brother, and friends and soaking in the natural beauty of the island that had always been a source of peace for me. During this time, I also opened a recording studio on Kaua'i and signed a publishing deal with a company that required me to deliver original songs.

At first, the task seemed daunting, but I looked forward to it. Writing had always been therapeutic for me, a way to process emotions and experiences that I couldn't quite articulate in other ways. Creating music every day also became a way for me to stay in an inspired state of mind, which always energized and motivated me. There was something about the quiet of Kaua'i, the sounds of the wind, rain, and ocean, and the tranquility of the island that fostered creativity in a way that I hadn't experienced in the hustle and bustle of city life.

I had never produced the music on my demos before, and this new challenge pushed me to grow in ways I hadn't anticipated. Because I needed to write, arrange, and produce a long list of songs and complete them relatively quickly, I forced myself to learn to create and arrange music. What started as a necessity soon became a passion. I found myself immersed in the technical aspects of music-making, spending hours experimenting with different sounds and arrangements, learning from every mistake, and celebrating every small victory. After two years of this, I realized I had become a far better writer, keyboardist, and guitarist than I ever was before. I had grown not just as an artist but as a person, finding a deeper connection to my craft and a renewed sense of purpose.

It was right about this time that I received a phone call from my manager that completely surprised me. Elton John, one of my musical idols, was involved in a situation that I could never have anticipated. Elton John has always been one of my favorite singers and songwriters. I studied his music inside out, both lyrically and musically, for many years. I considered him, and I still do today, as one of the finest musicians to ever live. His ability to craft songs that were both deeply personal and universally resonant had always inspired me. Although I didn't know Elton John very well, I did have the chance to sit across from him at Babyface's birthday party in Los Angeles—a surreal moment that

I'll never forget. We were also on the same recording labels both in the United States and throughout the rest of the world, with MCA Records here in the United States and Polygram Records internationally. Because of this, we had access to each other's music. Whenever we visited the offices of the record labels, we had access to stacks of our records and those of other artists, free for the taking. That's how I ended up with a CD copy of every one of Elton's albums.

All of this came rushing back to me when my manager told me over the phone that the song "Can You Feel the Love Tonight" sounded very much like a song I wrote on one of my records called "Listen to Your Heart." I had written that song in a studio in Connecticut when I was looking for one more track to complete the album. At first, I couldn't believe it. I had always admired Elton for his originality and his ability to create music that was unmistakably his own. However, when I put both songs side by side, the melody of the verses was almost identical. The similarity was undeniable. This realization led to my record/publishing company hiring an attorney to look into the situation, along with my own attorney for many years, Mark Bernstein. Soon after, our legal team hired two separate musicologists, experts in the field of music analysis, to compare the two songs. Both of their reports stated that there was a 99 percent chance that the melody to "Can You Feel the Love Tonight" had been lifted from the song I wrote.

After hearing this news, I was faced with a difficult decision. I was asked if I would participate in the legal process, which would likely require Elton John to take part in a deposition to determine whether he had created his song before I recorded mine. The idea of participating in this process put a really bad taste in my mouth. I didn't want to be seen as someone who was attacking a legend, especially one I had admired for so long. However, I was told by everyone around me—my manager, the attorneys, even close friends—that if the musicologists were correct, it was only fair for me to receive compensation for my original work. Long story short, I chose to move forward with my manager's plan, though with a heavy heart. The situation was even covered in *The New York Times*, a fact that added a surreal layer to the entire experience.

But in the end, I received a phone call one day stating that there wasn't enough evidence to prove that the melody was taken from my song. The case was closed, and I was left with mixed emotions. At that point in my music career, nothing surprised me anymore. I had learned that the music industry could be as unpredictable as it was exciting. Our attorneys were dealing with lawyers from Disney, one of the wealthiest and most powerful organizations in media. I did not expect the situation to work out in my favor. In fact, it made perfect sense that Elton might have heard the song I wrote and subconsciously remembered the melody without even realizing it. I can tell you that I've done that before as a writer—several songs were thrown out as soon as I discovered that they bore too strong a resemblance to something else. It's a common occurrence in songwriting, where melodies and ideas often float in the collective consciousness, influencing us in ways we don't always notice.

At the very least, I can say that I wrote something similar to one of the greatest writers who ever lived, and that was enough for me to feel that I'd come a long way as a musician. The experience, though challenging, reminded me of the interconnectedness of creativity.

Reflecting on this chapter of my life, I realize that these experiences, though difficult at the time, were crucial in shaping me into the artist and person I am today. They taught me resilience, the importance of authenticity, and the value of staying grounded, even when navigating the often turbulent waters of the music industry. As I moved forward, I carried these lessons with me, determined to continue creating music that was true to who I was and to share my journey with others, no matter where it led me.

Chapter 11

BEST LAID PLANS

In 1994, I was twenty-four years old and had done all I could to prepare myself for another shot in the music industry. After spending two years away from the spotlight, I felt fully energized, ready to dive back into the world that had been my life since I was sixteen. My ability to write music and play instruments had improved dramatically during those years, making me better prepared than ever for a successful comeback. I planned to move to Los Angeles, immerse myself in the music scene, and secure another record deal. This time, I decided to live in L.A. instead of constantly flying back and forth between L.A. and Hawaii. I had already moved out of my home and started renting it out, intending to stay with my parents for a few weeks before making the big move. After two to three years, I planned to return to Hawaii to go to college and begin a second career as an educator. But just a week into living with my parents, I received a phone call from local comedy legend Frank DeLima that would change the course of my life.

I first met Frank DeLima, one of Hawaii's most successful comedians, as a student at Koloa Elementary School. He visited our school yearly to talk to us about making good decisions, avoiding trouble, and being a kind, decent person. Of course, he intertwined those lessons with his signature humor—funny jokes, stories, and songs that had us all in stitches. Since elementary school, I had collected all of Frank's records and memorized most of his jokes. To me, Frank was one of the few Portuguese-Americans from Hawaii who had become a very successful entertainer, and I admired him immensely. After one of his presentations at Koloa School, I mustered up the courage to ask my teacher if I could get his autograph. I was a pretty shy kid for the most part, but singing had given me the confidence to be more outgoing, and this was one of the first times I had acted on that newfound courage. I ran to the parking lot, hoping to catch him before he left. Frank was incredibly kind. He not only gave me his autograph but also invited me and my dad to his show, offering us tickets. After his concert, we had a chance to chat, and when he found out that I could sing, he made a point to invite me to his shows on Kaua'i, even letting me perform occasionally. Frank became another mentor in my life, someone who saw potential in me and did everything he could to help me succeed.

When Frank called that day, I expected to have to tell him that I couldn't make it to his show because I would be on the mainland for the next couple of years. However, he surprised me with an opportunity that made me rethink my plans. Loyal Garner, another of Hawaii's beloved entertainers, needed a partner for her show in Waikiki. Her singing partner and good friend, Melveen Leed, had gotten married and was moving to Tahiti, leaving an unexpected opening. I was shocked because my mind was set on leaving for L.A., but I've always tried to stay open to signs from God, messages that might guide me in a different direction. After some thought, I realized that perhaps this was a sign that it was time to start my journey as an educator. The pay was good, and I could attend college during the day while performing at night. It didn't take long for me to say yes.

Soon after moving to Oahu, I was introduced to Fran Kirk, the Director of Entertainment at Outrigger Hotels. Fran was widely respected in the entertainment industry in Hawaii, particularly for her work with the Society of Seven and many other artists in Honolulu's showrooms. She believed I could be a draw as a performer in Waikiki and, along with Loyal Garner, took me under her wing. Both women taught me the ropes of being a showroom entertainer, which was very different from performing in large venues where crowds already knew and loved my music. In a nightclub setting, you had to earn the audience's appreciation. I remember Loyal telling me that when playing in clubs, finding dependable musicians was more important than finding the best ones. Reliability, she stressed, was more critical than talent—a far cry from my previous experiences, where talent had always been the priority. Fran and Loyal also took the time to create custom-made clothing for my performances, ensuring that I looked the part. They were so well organized that all I had to do was show up, perform five nights a week, and focus on honing my craft. Although I thoroughly enjoyed performing with Loyal, one of the most talented entertainers I've ever worked with, our show didn't attract large crowds. After about a year, Fran Kirk came up with a new idea that would bring Frank and me together on stage for our own show.

In the summer before our show opened, Fran paired me with Henry Kapono for a summer gig. Henry was a gentle, kind man, and working with him was a pleasure. Our show was all about the music—no skits, no comedy, just pure musical expression. It was basically a jam session, and while I enjoyed it, we once again struggled to draw large audiences. As I performed with Henry, I began preparing for the show with Frank DeLima, which we affectionately called "Pocho Knights." With both of us being Portuguese-American, we crafted a musical comedy show that played to our shared heritage and sense of humor.

Frank always had a strong following, but adding me to the show brought a fresh dynamic that drew audiences to see him again. For about three years, our showrooms were packed, and we performed skits written by Frank's friend and writer, Patrick Downes. Patrick was incredible when it came to writing comedic material and original songs, and the show was a hit. I looked forward to performing every night because the audience's laughter was infectious—there was something magical about knowing that we were making people's evenings memorable. Frank and I became even closer during those years. Not only did we share the same ethnic background and sense of humor, but we were also both Catholic and often shared our thoughts on faith before and after our shows. Today, Frank is the godfather of my two children, and he has truly been there for them, embodying that role with love and dedication.

As the years passed, I realized that my time in Waikiki would not last forever, and I began to focus on my education. I wanted to be prepared for the next chapter of my life, so I made it a priority to graduate from college as soon as possible. The first challenge was deciding where to go. I had never taken the SAT, and I hadn't been in school for six years. As I looked around, it became clear that my best option was community college. Leeward Community College (LCC) had a late registration date and hadn't already started its semester, so I enrolled there.

I'll never forget standing in line to register for classes. I was so nervous because, honestly, I didn't know if I had what it took to succeed in college. To many, this might sound odd, but I felt completely out of place. I had never fully committed myself academically, and the idea of returning to school after so many years filled me with anxiety. In retrospect, attending LCC was the best possible choice for me. The students there were a lot like me—people who hadn't necessarily excelled in school but were determined to make something of themselves. Once I began my studies, I noticed something that surprised me: I was the one people came to for help. This was a new experience for me, and it boosted my confidence in ways I hadn't expected. I believe my age and life experiences set me apart, and I was able to bring a level of maturity and commitment to my studies that I hadn't had before.

I thrived at LCC. For the first time in my life, my grade point average was high, and with that came a newfound confidence in my academic abilities. I realized that I had a knack for connecting new information to things I already knew, a skill that had developed from years of traveling the world and learning about different cultures. My life as a young child didn't involve much reading or a variety of activities, so I had little base knowledge from which to draw. But now, learning was more enjoyable because I could make connections that made the material come alive. The professors at LCC were passionate about their subjects, and their enthusiasm was contagious. My time management skills had also improved significantly since high school. I planned my study time carefully, ensuring that I stayed on top of my work. Additionally, advances in technology made studying easier—computers had replaced the typewriters of my high school days, making writing papers and completing assignments far less daunting.

My first goal was to complete my Associate's Degree successfully. When I did, I decided to study history, my favorite subject, with the aim of eventually earning a Master's Degree in Education. During my two years at LCC, I met several fantastic professors, but my favorite by far was Dr. Dan Boylan, my history professor. He was incredibly bright, passionate about history, and had a great sense of humor that made his classes a joy to attend. With his guidance and my determination, I was able to complete my BA in Humanities at UH West Oahu with a specialization in history within a year, earning 21 credits per semester and taking summer courses at both the University of Hawaii and UH West Oahu.

Juggling college during the day and performing at night left me with little time for anything else. But then, I met Tammy, who would soon become my wife.

We hit it off immediately, and everything about our relationship felt easy and natural. We spent countless hours together, talking about our future—our faith, our dreams of having children, and the roles we would play as parents. It was exciting to share our hopes and dreams and to find someone who shared my values but also complimented me with her unique personality. Beyond her beauty, Tammy had an incredible sense of humor that made every moment we spent together enjoyable. After just a few months, I knew she was the one I wanted to spend the rest of my life with. To everyone's surprise, we opted for a small, intimate wedding, choosing to save our money for a home instead. I thank God every day for bringing Tammy into my life.

In the late 1990s, the nightclub scene in Waikiki began to slow down, with luau shows becoming more popular. After purchasing our home in Mililani, my plan was to start teaching and work on my Master's Degree in Education. But life had other plans. I received an unexpected call from my friend Angie LaPrete, who had previously worked with me on a video for an original song I co-wrote and sang called "Kaua'i Aloha" during Hurricane Iniki. She told me that *Baywatch* was coming to Hawaii and that they needed a Music

Director. The news thrilled me—I had always wanted to work behind the scenes in television or film. After interviewing with the show's creator, I decided to put my teaching career on hold to take the job as Music Director for Baywatch Hawaii.

The job paid well, but it was demanding, involving long days and nights working with the show's producers and directors. My role involved reaching out to record labels and publishing companies, requesting songs to consider for each episode. After watching each episode and matching music to the scenes, I would present the selected songs to the producers and directors, who would make the final decisions. Once the music was chosen, I was responsible for coordinating the agreements between the publishing companies, writers, and Baywatch Hawaii to ensure the music was legally cleared for television.

The first season was an incredible experience, but I couldn't shake the feeling that Hawaii's own music deserved to be featured on the show. In my second year as Music Director, I was fortunate that the producer and new directors agreed with me. They had begun exploring Hawaii's local music scene and were impressed by the talent they found. To make this vision a reality, I needed to put the right structure in place. I introduced the producers of Baywatch Hawaii to several different local musicians who were producers and writers, and they asked me to reach out to Carlos Villalobos, a friend and collaborator. Carlos was a multi-talented musician from Chicago who also produced records in Hawaii. He could write, arrange, produce, and engineer quality music quickly—a necessity when working on a tight schedule of producing one episode per week. I also met with Baywatch Hawaii executives to secure a budget that would fairly compensate the local artists we wanted to feature. The show's budget was tight, but in the end, we managed to make it work. However, there was a catch: the show would only approve using local music if they owned the publishing rights, meaning the writing had to be done as work for hire. Carlos and I agreed to write the songs ourselves.

In that final year of Baywatch Hawaii, I had the privilege of working with some of Hawaii's most talented artists, including Keali'i Reichel and Fiji, to name a few. The songs we created together were something I was truly proud of. We even had the chance to work with Jason Momoa, who starred in the show.

When Baywatch Hawaii came to an end, I heard about a Department of Education program that allowed teachers in training to work while earning their Master's Degree in Special Education. I was living in Mililani at the time and was fortunate enough to land my first teaching job at Mililani Middle School as a Special Education teacher. Writing over twenty Individual Education Plans (IEPs) for my students was a daunting task for a first-year teacher, but it was a valuable learning experience. During my time there, I co-wrote the school's alma mater with another teacher, which is still in use today.

Teaching at Mililani Middle School was wonderful, but it quickly became clear that teaching was very different from performing. Unlike an audience, students see you every day, making it much more challenging to keep them engaged. The key to success in teaching, I learned, was good lesson planning, making real connections with students, and being a lifelong learner committed to growing as an educator. My experience at Mililani Middle School was brief but invaluable. However, as I reflected on my time in public education, I realized that something was missing. Having attended public schools my entire life, I had always believed in their value, but I began to see that the spiritual and faith elements that had been so important to me were absent. My faith had been a cornerstone of my life, and I felt strongly that the students I worked with could benefit from God's message in their lives.

I realized that my heart was guiding me toward something more. I wanted to teach in an environment where I could openly share the values that had shaped me and where I could help students not only academically but also spiritually. However, as a public school teacher, I was legally bound to keep my faith separate from my work. This realization led me to consider teaching at a Catholic school, where I could integrate my faith into my teaching and share it with my students. The idea of teaching at a Catholic school began to take root in my mind, and I knew that to make this transition, I needed to further my education and earn a Master's Degree in Education.

The decision to pursue this new path wasn't just about advancing my career—it was about aligning my work with my beliefs, about finding a place where I could be my authentic self in every aspect of my life. I was ready to embrace the next chapter of my journey, one that would combine my passion for teaching with my deep-rooted faith. The stage had been a wonderful place to grow, learn, and connect with others, but now, a new kind of stage was calling me—a classroom where I could make a lasting difference in the lives of my students, nurturing their minds and spirits.

Chapter 12

MR. M

My first true experience as a teacher came at Mililani Middle School, a place that marked the beginning of my educational journey. While teaching there, I pursued a Master's Degree in Special Education. However, after completing several classes, I came to a pivotal realization. Although special education teachers make an immense difference in the lives of students, I noticed that the classroom teacher often holds the most significant influence over a child's educational experience. This prompted me to switch to a Master's Degree in Elementary Education. The decision wasn't easy, but deep down, I felt I could make a bigger impact as a general education teacher.

I chose the University of Phoenix-Hawaii (UOP) for practical reasons. Their class schedules—Wednesday nights and Sundays—fit perfectly with my weekly performances. Looking back, I'm glad I chose UOP because it was more than just an academic institution; it was a place where I connected both online and in person with educators, counselors, and administrators who shared real-world knowledge during weekly class sessions. Their advice was invaluable. One of my classmates, a teacher at Saint Joseph School in Waipahu, mentioned that they were looking for a new music teacher. Intrigued, I applied, and before long, I found myself starting a new chapter as their music teacher the following school year.

Teaching at Saint Joseph School, a K-8 Catholic school, was a stark contrast to Mililani Middle School. With only 350 to 400 students, the close-knit atmosphere gave the school a family-like feel. There were about twenty-five teachers, along with a principal and vice principal, which made the administrators much more accessible. I could simply walk into their offices to share ideas or discuss concerns. It wasn't just the smaller size that set Saint Joseph apart; it was the school's deep commitment to faith. We prayed before and after meetings, attended retreats, and were constantly encouraged to integrate faith into our daily lives. Although

I had never attended a Catholic school myself, I felt a strong connection to the faith shared by everyone there. Mililani had been a great experience, but Saint Joseph felt like home—a place I needed at that stage of my life.

One of the best aspects of Saint Joseph was the openness of its leadership. Beverly Sandoval and the late Diane Esdicul were approachable and always ready to listen to ideas about faith or education. One day, while passing by the vice principal's office, I noticed them having lunch together. I hadn't yet found a comfortable spot for lunch since the teacher's lounge was often crowded. After a few more casual run-ins with the two administrators, they began inviting me to join them for lunch. What started as an occasional gathering soon became a daily occurrence. I didn't realize it at the time, but these lunches were the first step in my journey toward becoming an administrator. We discussed school challenges, strategies, and faith-based initiatives—all while sharing laughter. That laughter was vital in such a demanding job. Teaching doesn't come with the best pay or perks, but the joy we shared made the tough days easier to handle.

As a music teacher, I was fortunate to teach students from Pre-K to eighth grade. Each age group brought its own set of challenges and opportunities. I experimented with different teaching methods, introducing my students to singing, percussion instruments, and ukulele, and even started a small band. However, my proudest achievement during my time at Saint Joseph was a project in which each grade level wrote and performed their own original Christmas song. I helped arrange the music at home and brought my equipment to school to record their voices. We held a concert where they performed their songs, and afterward, we sold CDs. We raised several thousand dollars for the school's music program. It was an experience that blended creativity, teamwork, and music—and it wouldn't have been possible without the support of the administration.

As much as I loved teaching music, it became time for me to complete my Master's Degree in Elementary Education. The administrators at Saint Joseph graciously adjusted my schedule so I could spend part of my week working as a fifth-grade teacher. Under the mentorship of a master teacher whose motto was "Work smarter, not harder," I experienced immense growth. She was meticulous in her planning, always prepared, and her years of experience shone through in every lesson. My three months as a student-teacher under her guidance improved my teaching immensely, solidifying my belief that I had chosen the right path.

During that time, my conversations with the principal and vice principal often centered around students who struggled academically. We were determined to find ways to provide them with more support. The principal and I applied for a grant to attend a certification program in North Carolina run by Dr. Mel Levine, a Harvard graduate who specialized in educational neuroscience. We were accepted, and what followed was the most outstanding professional development opportunity of my career. Dr. Levine's Schools Attuned program was designed to help teachers understand how students learn and how to tailor interventions and accommodations to their specific needs. The program synthesized years of research into a practical framework that could be applied in the classroom.

Once we completed the rigorous certification, we were able to return to Saint Joseph and train our colleagues in the Schools Attuned method. The training empowered us to assess and accommodate students' diverse learning needs. The principal and I trained teachers across Hawaii's Catholic schools for the next three summers, sharing this life-changing educational approach.

Our daily lunch conversations soon began focusing on how to apply what we learned from Schools Attuned to Saint Joseph's students. The principal approached me one day and asked if I would like to take on the role of S.M.A.R.T. Coordinator—Students Making a Real Turn. I accepted immediately, knowing this was an opportunity to truly make a difference. I worked with about forty students, assessing their strengths and weaknesses and creating individualized learning plans. I also met with them during the school day, after school, and even on Saturdays. Over time, clear patterns emerged: many of these students were socially adept, athletically talented, artistic, and had a strong sense of spatial awareness. Yet, these very skills often led to distractions in the classroom. They struggled with time management, working memory, and higher-order thinking.

To address these challenges, I created plans that leveraged their strengths while addressing their areas for growth. Some strategies worked better than others, but the progress was often significant. One of the key lessons I imparted to these students was metacognition—

understanding how they learned best. Once they grasped this concept, many of them began to thrive. It was deeply fulfilling to watch these students develop into lifelong learners. The growth I made as an educator in this period of my life was immense. I could not have done that without the mentorship of Beverly Sandobal, the school's principal, and Diane Esdical, the vice principal, two amazing Catholic school leaders.

During this period, two life-changing events occurred—the births of my children, Chord and Lyric. Becoming a father brought with it a strong sense of responsibility. Suddenly, my thoughts shifted to the future—saving for private school, planning for college, and ensuring that I could provide for my family. Tammy and I discussed our roles and agreed that she would focus on raising the kids while I worked to support us financially. This meant taking on more jobs if necessary. Though I loved my work at Saint Joseph, I eventually realized that I needed to earn more to support my growing family, which led me to accept a position at Island Pacific Academy (IPA), a new non-Catholic private school that offered a higher salary.

My transition to IPA was both exciting and intriguing. The school was only a couple of years old, and

I joined as a teacher and curriculum coordinator. I quickly learned that creating a new private school in a very competitive private school environment in Hawaii was not easy. Many of the families wanted more than just academics—they wanted a gym, a field, and extracurricular activities that would give their children a well-rounded experience. Unfortunately, enrollment began dropping, and I began to look at other, more established Catholic schools in town. Despite the school experiencing the need to make adjustments as new schools often do, my time at IPA was invaluable. I honed my teaching skills, grew as a curriculum coordinator, and began to see the broader picture of what it meant to be an administrator. Working closely with the Head of School, Dr. Dan White, and his wife, the Admissions Director, I learned the importance of aligning a school's mission with the needs of its families. It wasn't enough to have a vision—you needed to ensure that vision resonated with your community. IPA may have been a young school, but it was a fantastic place to learn and grow, not only for its students but also for me personally.

My time at IPA helped me realize that I should seriously consider becoming an administrator. The experience I gained working with students from Pre-K to twelfth grade prepared me for the next steps in my career. Eventually, I would become a Dean of Academics, a Vice Principal, and later, a Principal and School President. Along the way, I was fortunate to have mentors who believed in me and saw beyond my background as a singer when I was hired as a history teacher at Maryknoll School. One of those mentors was Betsey Gunderson, who played a pivotal role in supporting my growth. I owe so much to her and others who believed in me, and I can never fully repay them for their faith in my abilities.

However, my last year at IPA brought with it an immense personal challenge—the passing of my father. My father had lived a life full of indulgences—cigarettes, beer, and rich food—which had taken a toll on his body. Though he had undergone successful heart bypass and throat surgery, his health began to decline in his late sixties. His movements became stiff, and soon he could no longer speak or walk. Watching my father's health deteriorate was the hardest thing I have ever experienced. He had always told me how much he regretted not being there when his father passed away while he served our country as a Marine in Korea, and he made me promise that I would be with him in his final moments. Thankfully, God granted him that wish. I was able to be there by his side as he took his last breath.

After my father passed, I experienced a deep sense of loss I had never felt before. The grief was overwhelming, and I found it difficult to function. I could barely leave the house for weeks without feeling anxious or overwhelmed. Slowly, the intense pain began to fade, and I found my way back to some sense of normalcy. But the experience left a lasting impact on me. My mother, who had cared for him tirelessly, became a beacon of strength in those difficult months. Her devotion to him in his final days remains one of the most powerful examples of love I have ever witnessed.

In the months following his death, I knew I needed a change. My father had always been there for me, and his absence left a void that I couldn't ignore. I also longed to return to a Catholic school environment where faith was a central part of daily life. Around this time, a history teaching position opened at Maryknoll School, a private, coeducational Catholic school serving children in kindergarten through twelfth grade in

Honolulu. I saw this as an opportunity to re-center myself, both personally and professionally. And it felt like the perfect fit. And so, with a renewed sense of purpose, I stepped onto the next stage of my life.

Chapter 13

MR. MEDEIROS

Walking into Maryknoll School for the first time, I knew deep down that I wanted to make a more significant impact on students' lives. I had a growing desire to become an administrator who could shape a school's broader vision. But like most things in my life, I trusted that God would guide me to the right place and the right time. For now, my primary goal was simple: be the best teacher I could be.

Under the leadership of Betsey Gunderson, our principal, I found myself in an environment that truly valued professional development. The culture at Maryknoll was one where teachers were constantly encouraged to grow and improve. There were seasoned educators all around me—teachers who were so deeply loved by their students that watching students learn under them became an inspiring experience. I watched closely, learning not just from my own experiences but from the master teachers around me.

When I taught at the elementary level, I enjoyed the energy and curiosity of young students. But I found the subject matter somewhat limited—after all, I was teaching the basics. When I moved into teaching high school history, everything changed. The depth and complexity of the content were incredibly engaging, and it reignited my passion for teaching. But with that complexity came new challenges. Teaching high school students was no easy task. Unlike elementary kids who would give you a hug and forget any misunderstandings by the next day, high school students could be more sensitive. Missteps weren't easily forgotten.

Still, after some time, I found my rhythm as a high school teacher. By my fourth year of teaching history, I had begun to achieve the kind of instruction I had always envisioned. I saw substantial growth in my students, not just in their knowledge but in their skills. We started each class with prayer, and I made a habit of asking my students for their special intentions. Those moments of reflection gave me a window into their emotional lives, allowing me to tailor my teaching to their needs on a deeper level. Whether it was honing their persuasive writing, teaching them to present confidently in AP U.S. History, or challenging my students in various ways to express themselves creatively using their own talents and affinities when answering essential questions, I felt like I had finally hit my stride as an educator. Just as I was reaching that point, I received a life-changing opportunity. I was asked to interview for the vice principal position at Maryknoll Elementary School and was fortunate enough to be hired by its principal, Shana Tong!

There were many talented candidates for the vice principal position, and because I had been teaching at the high school, I wasn't sure if I would be given the opportunity. Although Maryknoll's Elementary and High schools were technically part of the same institution, they were on separate campuses and had their own distinct cultures. When I found out I had been chosen, it was a moment of disbelief, followed by gratitude. I immediately thought back to how unprepared I had been when I first entered my singing career. That had been a whirlwind, and it taught me the value of preparation. This time, however, I had put in years of hard work to build a solid foundation as a SMART Coordinator, Curriculum Coordinator, and teacher.

Stepping into the vice principal role marked a new chapter in my journey—a shift from teacher to leader. And I knew instinctively that if I was going to be successful, I needed to prepare myself further. I considered attaining a second Master's Degree but eventually decided that a doctorate in leadership would give me the skills I needed to navigate the complexities of school administration. I researched different programs and eventually set my sights on the University of Southern California's (USC) doctoral program in Educational Leadership. For the first time in my life, I tested and interviewed for a competitive academic program, hoping to be accepted.

When I received the acceptance letter, it felt surreal. Growing up, I had always watched USC and Notre Dame football games on TV. Although my family leaned toward Notre Dame because of our Catholic roots, being accepted into USC felt like stepping into something bigger than myself. I wasn't just watching from the sidelines—I was becoming part of the Trojan family. And I wanted nothing more than to prove to them and to myself that I deserved to be there.

The following two years as vice principal at Maryknoll's Elementary School were extraordinary. But they also introduced me to the reality of administrative life—long hours, constant problem-solving, and the need to balance multiple priorities. As a teacher, I had already been working long hours grading papers and preparing lessons. But as an administrator, the workload doubled. Balancing my administrative duties with the demands of the USC doctoral program was no small feat. Writing long research papers while managing a school could be overwhelming at times, but I was determined. Tammy's support during this time was invaluable. She took care of the kids the majority of the time, giving me the time and space to focus on my work and studies.

The courses at USC were phenomenal. The professors flew in from Los Angeles every two weeks, ensuring that we were getting the same quality education as students on campus. I could feel the immediate impact of what I was learning in my day-to-day work at Maryknoll. The educational concepts and theories I studied aligned with the challenges I faced as an administrator, giving me a unique advantage in both my assignments and my role at the school.

After two years under the guidance of another wonderful leader, Principal Shana Tong, an opportunity came my way. The new high school principal, Darcie Kawamura, approached me with an offer to join her as Vice Principal. Darcie had been the vice principal for many years and was now stepping into her new role as principal. Although I had grown attached to the elementary school, I knew this was an opportunity to gain experience in high school administration—an environment that brought its own set of challenges, including managing credits, schedules, transcripts, and college applications. My leadership journey was a natural progression, and I couldn't pass it up.

Returning to the high school, this time as an administrator, was a different experience. Being a teacher there, I noticed a subtle change in how some of my colleagues interacted with me. It's only natural—people tend to be more cautious around administrators, knowing that their words and actions might carry more weight. It was a good lesson for me to learn early on in my administrative career. The higher you move up the leadership ladder, the lonelier it can become. My priority was earning the trust of the faculty, ensuring that they knew I was working to create the best environment for them to thrive. Trust, like any relationship, takes time to build, and I was prepared to earn it.

When I finally completed my doctorate, it was an incredible milestone. As much as I loved being vice principal at Maryknoll, I realized I was ready for the next challenge. There weren't any immediate leadership openings at Maryknoll, so I began to explore the possibility of transitioning to higher education. The idea of becoming a college professor and eventually an administrator at that level appealed to me. When I saw that Chaminade University was looking for a Professor of Education with a specialization in history, I knew I had to apply.

The interview process went smoothly, and to my delight, I was offered the position. In hindsight, the move to Chaminade was the right decision for me and my family. My years at Maryknoll had shaped me into the leader and educator I had become, and I would always hold a deep love for the people there, especially the Maryknoll Sisters. Their spirit of service and the school's motto, *Noblesse Oblige*—to whom much is given, much is expected—continue to inspire me to use the gifts God has given me to help others.

At Chaminade, I found new challenges and opportunities. The shift from high school to college-level teaching was significant, but it allowed me to explore education from a broader perspective. I also began to understand the intricacies of higher education. While I missed the daily interaction with younger students, the work I did with college students hoping to become educators was very fulfilling.

Whether as a teacher, administrator, or professor, I found my greatest joy in serving my students, colleagues, and community. Every step I took, whether forward or backward, was guided by faith in God, myself, and others. I believe that each role I held prepared me for the next stage in ways I couldn't have anticipated. God's timing, as always, was perfect.

Chapter 14

BECOMING PRESIDENT

Working as a full-time professor at Chaminade University was a deeply rewarding experience. My days were filled with teaching, crafting lesson plans, and preparing for the first time at a college level, but they were also enriched by special moments with my students. The classes at Chaminade were intentionally small, typically no more than ten to fifteen students, which meant that every student received individualized attention. I was able to connect with each one, guiding them not only through academic challenges but also in their faith, helping those who sought spiritual growth. Since the university was a Catholic Marianist college, the combination of intellectual and spiritual mentorship became deeply fulfilling, knowing I was helping shape the next generation of teachers who would make a difference in Hawaii's schools.

At first, it felt a bit strange being addressed as "Dr. Medeiros" by my students. I had spent so long as "Mr. M" or "Mr. Medeiros" that the title seemed almost foreign. But as time passed, I grew into it, recognizing it as a reflection of the hard work and dedication that had brought me to this point in my career. Chaminade was a special place where education wasn't just about learning facts and figures but about fostering a deeper connection with the community through service. My time at Chaminade University gave me another example of the combined power of faith and education.

While I was content at Chaminade, an unexpected opportunity arose when Dr. John Henry Felix, a well-respected leader and philanthropist, informed me about an opening at Saint Louis School. The position was for Head of School, and while Saint Louis had always been a prestigious institution, it had been facing significant challenges in recent years. Enrollment had dropped, and the school's future was uncertain. It was a daunting prospect, but the topic of helping Hawaii's Catholic schools was something I had written about in my dissertation, and the possibility of putting that research into practice intrigued me.

I hadn't known Dr. Felix very well before this opportunity, though I had seen him at various board meetings during my time at Maryknoll School. I always admired his quiet, observant nature—he seemed to listen more than he spoke. One day, Dr. Felix approached me directly and expressed his belief that I had what it took to be the next leader of Saint Louis School. Coming from someone with a background in servant leadership, this was high praise, and I felt both honored and humbled. He eventually became a mentor to me, offering guidance and support throughout my career as a leader.

The interview process for the Head of School position was long and rigorous, taking several months. With no prior ties to Saint Louis School, I knew being chosen there was a long shot. But to my surprise, one day, I received the call that I had been selected as the new Head of School at Saint Louis. It was a thrilling moment, tempered by the knowledge that the road ahead would not be easy. Saint Louis was at a crossroads, and I knew I would be stepping into a role that required difficult decisions.

One of my first tasks was to meet with the outgoing president of Saint Louis, the Honorable Judge Walter Kirimitsu, a kind and intelligent man who had worked tirelessly to serve his alma mater. He had dedicated ten years to the school, but Saint Louis was struggling despite his efforts. Nonetheless, enrollment had dropped to the high 400s just a few years earlier, though it had rebounded somewhat to around 600 students shortly before I was hired, largely due to the media attention surrounding Heisman Trophy winner and Saint Louis graduate Marcus Mariota. Yet, even with that boost, it was clear that the school was still on shaky ground. Saint Louis faced significant financial challenges, and I quickly realized that without careful management, the school could face closure.

The board decided that instead of having both a president and principal, the two roles would be combined into a single position—Head of School. It was a practical decision aimed at saving money and simplifying the chain of command. With all final decisions directed by one person, we could act swiftly and decisively, which was crucial given the urgency of the situation.

One of my first major actions as the head of the school was reducing personnel costs by approximately $500,000. It was a painful process involving letting go of staff members who had dedicated themselves to the school. These were people who had played important roles at Saint Louis for many years, but in the face of financial necessity, their positions were no longer sustainable. I also had to take a hard look at our programs. On my first day, the CFO of the school quit, leaving me with the grim news that we didn't have enough money for the next payroll. The advice given to me by a few administrators was to cut the JROTC program, which they felt was too much of a financial burden. As a member of a cadet program myself, I was deeply conflicted. The JROTC had a rich history at Saint Louis, and I knew it was important to many students and alumni. However, the financial reality was hard to ignore.

Initially, I made the tough decision to suspend the JROTC program for one year, hoping to bring it back once we were on more stable financial footing. The backlash from parents and students was immediate and intense. Many saw the decision as a sign that I didn't understand or appreciate the school's traditions.

What struck me, however, was the way the students responded. Groups of cadets came to my office not to protest or complain but to respectfully ask if there was a way to save the program. They presented solutions, offered compromises, and showed a level of maturity and dedication that deeply impressed me.

After further consideration and conversations with the board and alumni, I reversed my decision and kept the JROTC program running. This decision wasn't just about finances or tradition—it was about listening to the students and recognizing the value they placed on the program. In many ways, it was a turning point in my early days as Head of School. People began to see me as someone who was willing to listen and adapt rather than a distant administrator making decisions without input from others.

However, the financial challenges didn't end there. In addition to releasing personnel and finding ways to save on programs, we also froze a recently introduced benefit that offered free tuition to the nephews and grandchildren of employees. It was another difficult decision, but one that was necessary to keep the school afloat. At the same time, I had to finalize the sale of a dormitory and office building, a process initiated by my predecessor. Selling Hale Hoaloa to Chaminade University helped reduce the school's debt but created new challenges, as we had to quickly find space for the displaced programs and resources.

With the support of the board of trustees, the Marianists, the Saint Louis Alumni Association, and key donors like the Clarence T. C. Ching Foundation, we managed to make it through my first year as the Head of the School financially intact. It was a grueling process, but it set the stage for the school's recovery.

One of the most important strategic decisions we made was to expand our enrollment by adding an elementary school. While there was some initial hesitation about whether there would be enough interest to fill the classes, I firmly believed that this was the right path forward. We turned classrooms that had been used for storage into learning spaces, with significant financial support from alumni like Tony Guerrero and Dwight Otani, as well as donations from the Class of 1966.

The upgrade of Newell Hall into an elementary school was a grassroots effort. With the support of Michael Yee, a Stanford-educated engineer, Saint Louis School alumnus, and board member, along with his wife Chuen, one of Hawaii's top interior designers, we tackled the project together. They helped us repurpose old high school classrooms into functional spaces for elementary school students. Our hard work paid off, and by the start of the next school year, the new elementary school was ready to open on time.

The addition of the elementary school had an immediate and significant impact on our enrollment. In just one year, the student population grew from 631 to 832, with around 120 new students coming from the elementary grades. As we had hoped, many of these younger students had older brothers who also enrolled at Saint Louis, further boosting our numbers. This surge in enrollment provided a much-needed financial lifeline, and by the end of my second year, we began chipping away at millions of dollars of debt.

As the school continued to grow, the board decided to move me into the role of president and hire a new principal, allowing me to focus more on long-term strategic planning and fundraising. Over the next seven years, enrollment remained steady, hovering between 830 and 895 students. We continued to innovate, expanding our robotics program and improving our academic offerings to ensure that we weren't relying primarily on the success of athletics to attract students. Marcus Mariota's success on the national stage as a Heisman Trophy winner and quarterback in the National Football League kept Saint Louis School in the spotlight, but we knew we needed a solid plan to sustain the school's future.

One of the keys to success at Saint Louis School was the development of our robotics program. We transformed a storage room into a state-of-the-art robotics lab equipped with thousands of dollars worth of tools utilizing a grant that we had recently received. After hiring a very young and talented robotics teacher from another school who had achieved great success, our team began winning several robotics competitions and gaining recognition. This was a testament to the power of combining the right space, the right talent, and a commitment to excellence.

In addition to our academic successes, our athletics program also flourished. After years of effort, our basketball team won its first state championship in over three decades. The combination of a dedicated coaching staff, the leadership of our Athletics Committee, and the opening of the Clarence T. C. Ching Athletic Center created the perfect environment for success. Just a few years later, we celebrated our third consecutive Division One HHSAA State Championship in basketball.

Seven years into my time as President, Saint Louis School had transformed. Enrollment was strong, our endowment had grown immensely by millions of dollars, and we had eliminated the majority of our debt. The renovations of classrooms, the creation of new, multi-million dollar athletic facilities, and renovated playgrounds, along with the development of new programs, all played a part in revitalizing the school.

None of this would have been possible without the unwavering support of the faculty, staff, alumni, board members, my predecessor, Judge Kirimitsu, and the Marianist community. Their dedication, combined with the generosity of donors and the hard work of countless individuals, helped bring Saint Louis School back to its feet. As I look back on these achievements, I feel an immense sense of gratitude for the entire Saint Louis community. With the help of great alumni like Walter Dods, Tony Guerrero, Dwight Otani, Damien Farias, Merton Lau, Ray Tam, Robin Yoshimura, David Coleman, Dr. Greg Lung and non-graduates like Mike Hogan, Mike Irish, and Marlene De Costa, to name a few, and organizations like the Marianists, the Saint Louis Alumni Association, and the Clarence T. C. Ching Foundation, the prospect of eliminating our debt had become a reality and the future looked bright.

Chapter 15

PHOENIX

My favorite poet, Maya Angelou, once said, "Courage is the greatest of all virtues. You cannot have the others without courage." Reflecting on my life, I've come to understand that courage, more than anything else, has helped me persevere through challenging moments. Courage allowed me to face unexpected obstacles, embrace the victories, and learn from the failures. Throughout my life, I've been blessed with mentors who were guardian angels, pushing me to have faith in myself and to keep going even when the road ahead seemed uncertain. Their encouragement, paired with my belief that God has a plan and purpose for all of us, kept me focused through the highs and lows. This perseverance and constant renewal is why an old friend recently called me a "Phoenix." Like the mythical bird rising from its ashes, I've faced the fire and returned stronger.

After years of dedicating every ounce of energy to helping Saint Louis School recover and thrive, the positive energy surrounding our efforts began to change soon after the COVID-19 pandemic was over. Just as we successfully emerged from it, about seven years into my presidency, a new challenge was on the horizon that can be encapsulated into one word: politics. The average stay today for a private K-12 school leader is three to five years. Part of the reason for this is that when a certain number of decisions do not go the way some people want within an organization, whether it's hiring the person they wanted, outsourcing certain positions, or simply moving from one coach to another, over time, some become unhappy with those choices.

Unfortunately, when this occurs, instead of working with leadership transparently and collaboratively to solve disagreements, a group of dissenters will sometimes seek to destroy the leader's reputation, spreading mistruths about them. This unfortunate situation occurs more often than people think, especially in environments like schools, where there is much passion over decisions that impact our youth, teachers, coaches, and so on, and make for good news in the media. Nonetheless, most people can distinguish between the truth and fabricated lies. When people hide behind a mask of anonymity, that is usually a good sign that they are unwilling to stand behind their assertions.

Catholic schools across the United States are facing several challenges. Almost ten Catholic schools in Hawaii alone have closed in the past twenty years. The Catholic School model of education began in the 1800s, when fathers, brothers, and sisters worked at no cost, thus allowing Catholic schools to offer reasonable tuition rates for a population of people wanting a private school education for their children. Today, the cost of paying for lay educators and keeping their salaries competitive has caused tuition rates to spike. In addition, there are far fewer Catholics today than in the past, further causing enrollment to drop due to a lack of "feeder schools." Moreover, many Catholic schools have small endowments or none at all. Endowments in the form of scholarships can help to provide the financial help families need to afford to send their children to private Catholic schools.

At Saint Louis School, our endowment funds have grown by millions in the last decade, and we have also eliminated several million dollars of debt, making us currently debt-free. However, as with any private school, financial health can change quickly, so supporting enrollment by spreading positive news about its accomplishments and donations from alumni, parents, and students makes all the difference. With this in mind, we will soon begin our Century on Kalaepohaku Campaign, where we hope to renovate buildings approximately a century old and build a new stadium on campus. An initiative like this will require raising at least twenty-five to fifty million dollars. Still, we've done it before and can do it again when we work together as a team, regardless of the obstacles in the way of our Catholic schools in Hawaii.

As I look back on my decade-long tenure on the slopes of Kalaepohaku as the President of Saint Louis School, I am grateful for the people who helped make this Catholic Marianist educational institution what it is today. The alums have been an incredible source of inspiration and support. From philanthropists like Walter Dods and Dwight Otani to world-famous athletes like Marcus Mariota and Tua Tagovailoa, the

Saint Louis community has produced leaders who have impacted people here in Hawaii and worldwide. Even those who have passed on, like Clarence T.C. Ching and Tony Guerrero, have left legacies that continue to shape the school's future.

The Saint Louis Alumni Association, under the amazing leadership of Gregory Frey and Bobby Hall, played a pivotal role in the school's survival. When the school faced millions of dollars in debt, the Alumni Association used its clubhouse as collateral, ensuring that the school had the financial support it needed to stay open. Their dedication to the school and the Marianist mission has been nothing short of heroic.

Speaking of our Marianist Father and Brothers, I would be remiss if I didn't acknowledge their incredible role at Saint Louis School. The Marianist Fathers and Brothers have been the heart and soul of this institution since they saved it from closure in 1883. Their commitment to education, faith, and community has guided the school through its most challenging moments. I have been blessed to learn from so many Marianists—Brother John, Father Marty, Brother Jessie, Brother Ed, Brother Tom, Brother Bernie, the late Father Allen, Father Pat, and Larry Keller, to name just a few. Their wisdom, compassion, and faith have made me a better person, educator, and leader. The Marianist ohana is truly a family, and I am honored to be a part of it.

Looking ahead, I know that Saint Louis School's challenges are not over. We have moved from surviving toward thriving, but the road ahead will require continued vigilance, innovation, and courage. There will be new hurdles to overcome, new decisions, and new opportunities to seize. But I have faith—faith in the mission of Saint Louis School, the community that supports it, and the next generation of leaders who will carry the torch forward.

In my journey, I have learned that every challenge is an opportunity for growth. The moments of hardship and doubt, the times when it felt like we were on the brink of failure—these were the moments that shaped me as a leader and as a person. Through it all, I have understood that leadership is not about having all the answers but the courage to listen, adapt, and trust in the people around you.

In many ways, my journey at Saint Louis School has reflected the school's own story—one of perseverance, faith, and transformation. Like the Phoenix, we have risen from the ashes through adversity on several occasions in our 180-plus year history, not just to survive but to thrive. The work is far from over, and more challenges will undoubtedly be ahead. But with the proper focus, the right people, and the courage to face whatever comes next, I do not doubt that Saint Louis School will continue to make a difference in the lives of Hawaii's young men for generations to come.

Chapter 16

LESSONS I'VE LEARNED

In life, we learn lessons at every stage—lessons that shape our decisions, our worldview, and, ultimately, our understanding of life. I've come to realize that these lessons, learned through experience and reflection, have shaped how I navigate the challenges and opportunities that life presents. What I hope to convey in this chapter are some of the most significant lessons I've learned over the years.

These lessons weren't always easy. Some were hard-won through failure, disappointment, and moments of doubt. Others came through success and unexpected joy. What ties them all together is that each one contributed to my growth, helping me understand who I am, what I value, and what truly brings happiness.

From an early age, my family instilled in me the importance of faith, respect, and responsibility. On Kaua'i, where community and family were everything, the traditional values of hard work and dedication were emphasized above all else. The path to happiness, I was taught, was straightforward: believe in God, respect others, get a job, start a family, and serve others.

These values were deeply rooted in our culture. Growing up, I remember watching my parents work hard, not for wealth or recognition but to provide stability for the family. They didn't chase after dreams of fame or fortune. Instead, their focus was on ensuring we had enough—enough food on the table, enough love in the home, and enough security to keep us safe.

Looking back, I see that this simplicity provided a solid foundation for my life. It gave me a sense of security that many people take for granted. There's something to be said for the comfort of knowing that you have what you need. My parents were far from being wealthy, but they taught me the value of appreciating what you have and being satisfied with having enough to get by.

But as I got older, I began to question whether that path was the right one for me. The idea of finding happiness through stability, while valuable, left me wondering if there was more to life than what I'd been taught. This questioning wasn't a rejection of my upbringing but rather a desire to explore beyond the boundaries set for me.

The Teenage Years: The Allure of Fame

Like many teenagers, I began to dream of a bigger life—a life that went beyond the simplicity of my upbringing. Movies and television painted a picture of what appeared to be a more exciting, glamorous existence. These people on the big screen had money, admiration, and a lifestyle that seemed far more fulfilling than what I saw around me.

At that point, the path of becoming a teacher, as I had once imagined, started to feel limiting. Perhaps I could be something more. Perhaps I could achieve fame, wealth, and the kind of success that would elevate not only my life but also the lives of those around me. Success as a professional singer and writer, I thought, could be the key to unlocking a life of true purpose and fulfillment.

My love for singing became the vehicle for this dream. What started as a personal passion soon turned into something more as I began performing professionally. The adrenaline of being on stage, the admiration from the audience, and the fleeting moments of success made me feel as if I was on the right path.

This stage of my life taught me an important lesson about the nature of fame. On the surface, fame seems like the ultimate goal—the culmination of all your hard work and dreams. But once you reach that level, it becomes clear that fame is fleeting. The highs are high, but the lows are deep. Fame, I realized, could bring moments of joy, but it was artificial and wasn't enough to sustain long-term happiness.

The College Years: The Power of Education

As the years passed, the allure of fame began to wear off, and I found myself searching for something more stable, something that would provide a sense of long-term fulfillment. Enter the Wada family, who introduced me to the idea that education could offer the stability and freedom that fame never could.

At first, the idea of going to college seemed like a step back. After all, I had been living the life of a performer, experiencing highs that few of my peers had ever known. But as I began my educational journey, I realized that college wasn't just about getting a degree—it was about gaining the tools to shape my future.

The Wada family's guidance shifted my understanding of success. Mr. Wada once told me that while money doesn't bring happiness, it gives you the freedom to make choices. And that freedom—freedom to choose your path, to direct your life in the way you want—is invaluable. He also taught me that the two things he could provide his children that no one else could ever take away were love and an education. This life lesson deeply resonated with me.

College provided me with the structure, discipline, and confidence I needed to pursue a career that would sustain me and allow me to grow. It gave me the tools to make decisions based on my own values rather than the whims of the entertainment industry.

This period taught me the importance of investing in yourself—not just in terms of financial stability but in personal development. It showed me that education is about more than just knowledge; it's about creating opportunities and ensuring that you have the skills to adapt to whatever life throws your way.

Teaching: Making an Impact

After college, I became a teacher, fulfilling the dream I had once had as a child. Teaching became a calling, a way to give back and contribute to something greater than myself.

One of the most significant lessons I've learned from teaching is the value of impact. Every day, teachers have the opportunity to shape the minds and hearts of young people. It's not just about the curriculum—it's about teaching students how to think, solve problems, and navigate life's challenges.

The lessons I taught in the classroom extended far beyond academic subjects. I had the opportunity to inspire, to mentor, and to guide students toward becoming their best selves. The joy of seeing a student succeed and of watching them grow into confident, capable individuals was far more rewarding than anything fame had ever offered me.

But even as I found fulfillment in teaching, I began to realize that there was more I could do. I wanted to have a greater impact, to touch the lives of more people. This realization led me to the next stage of my journey: leadership.

Leadership brought its own set of challenges. As an administrator, I had the chance to influence the direction of an entire school, shape its future, and ensure the success of hundreds of students. But with that opportunity came the weight of that responsibility as a leader.

One of the greatest lessons I've learned in leadership is that decisions rarely make everyone happy. Sometimes, the right decision is the unpopular one, and that can feel incredibly isolating. Leadership requires a level of resilience and fortitude that I hadn't anticipated. It's not just about making the right choices—it's about standing by them, even when others don't understand all the variables considered when making tough decisions.

As a leader, I also learned the importance of balance. Leadership is a balancing act between competing demands—between what is best for the organization and what is best for the individuals within it. It's about finding a way to navigate these competing priorities without losing sight of the bigger picture.

At times, I struggled to find balance in my own life. The demands of leadership often meant long hours, stress, and pressure that affected my relationships and personal well-being. But through those challenges, I learned that balance is not about perfection—it's about finding harmony between the various aspects of life.

At each stage of my life, I see that each lesson has contributed to my growth. From the simple values of my upbringing, which taught me the importance of security and community, to the ambition and dreams of my teenage years, I've learned to embrace both stability and risk. The experiences I've had—whether in the classroom, on stage, or in the leadership role of an administrator—have shaped my understanding of what it means to live a fulfilling life.

These lessons are not isolated events. They are part of an ongoing journey of growth and self-discovery. What I've come to understand is that life isn't about reaching a final destination where everything falls perfectly into place. Instead, it's about continually evolving, learning, and becoming more aligned with who you truly are.

As I reflect on these experiences, I realize that leadership is as much about who you are on the inside as it is about what you do on the outside. The decisions, the balance, the resilience—it all stems from a deeper place: your mindset. Leadership begins not with strategy or titles but with the thoughts, beliefs, and habits that shape how you see yourself and the world around you. If you want to lead others well, you must first lead yourself with clarity and intention. That realization marked a turning point for me, where leadership became less about the role I held and more about the person I chose to become.

Chapter 17

FROM GOOD TO SUPERIOR

As I prepare for the final stages of my life, my desire to help others by providing for my family and giving back to my community continues to motivate my actions. For almost twenty years, I worked very hard to be the best leader I could be by utilizing past experiences, obtaining a doctorate in educational leadership, and attending various professional development conferences. Although these approaches have helped me become a better leader, I felt the need to do more. That is when I began looking more closely at the work of my good friend, Rusty Komori.

Rusty Komori is someone I've admired over the years. As Head Coach of the Punahou School Boys Varsity Tennis Team for twenty-two years, he led his teams to win twenty-two consecutive State Championships from 1994 to 2015. Since retiring as Head Coach, he's become a best-selling author and a highly sought-after Keynote Speaker and Executive Coach. I've read all three of his books, and I even added a brief snippet in his latest book, *Superior.*

Throughout the years, we met as friends and rarely discussed the strategies he has developed to help leaders reach their full potential. However, after completing the first sixteen chapters of my book, I felt the need to start sharing the next stage of my life—one focused on becoming a better leader. As I began speaking to Rusty more about the specific concepts he has developed, it became clear to me that the next stage in my journey of life would require a more personalized and consistent approach to learning about leadership and that Rusty was the perfect Executive Coach to take my leadership from where it is today to superior.

In the short time I've worked with Rusty in this capacity, I've been blown away by the depth of insight he brings to the table. His guidance has challenged me, inspired me, and reshaped how I view leadership. That's why I've chosen to write this final chapter as an open invitation—for you to step into the next phase of my journey with me. None of us can predict exactly what the future holds, but one thing is sure: the need for strong, values-driven leaders has never been greater. If sharing my path toward becoming that kind of leader can help spark something in someone else, then it's worth telling.

Rusty and I both believe that simplicity is key to learning and applying leadership principles. So, in this chapter, I'll share a few meaningful takeaways from our coaching conversations—insights that have helped me grow and that I hope will do the same for you.

Read and enjoy!

(Glenn)

"How do I master my mindset to take the organization I lead from good to superior?"

(Coach Rusty)

"I always say that there are two types of people in the world: one has a victim mindset, and the other has a victor mindset. People with a victim mindset often make excuses and blame others for the problems they're dealing with. People with a victor mindset focus on solutions and

approach setbacks as temporary obstacles while they look for ways to overcome those barriers.

"Glenn, you clearly demonstrated a victor mindset when you helped turn around Saint Louis School from the possibility of closing. You were forced to make very difficult decisions for the good of the school to ultimately keep Saint Louis School alive. It's entirely natural to second-guess your decisions—especially when criticism rolls in after the fact. But at the end of the day, you're the one who has to live with the outcomes, not the people offering their opinions. Glenn, what's clear to me is that your top priority has always been serving the people of Saint Louis School—and that's what truly matters.

"A big part of mastering your mindset is consistently being aware of your thoughts by taking time to self-reflect. It means regularly checking in with your thoughts through intentional self-reflection. From there, it's about actively reshaping those thoughts, beliefs, and perspectives to stay grounded in a victor mindset. I call this practice mental fitness. Just like we train our bodies to stay physically strong, we need to train our minds to stay mentally strong. Through habits like mindfulness and meditation, we build the resilience needed to handle life's challenges—

and it all begins with learning to guide, not just react to, our thoughts.

"I want you to have a mindset that welcomes adversity and looks forward to challenges. When you experience adversity, you become stronger and tougher because you dealt with it and got through it. All great leaders are tested, and you're a better person for experiencing that. So here's my reasoning: adversities are inevitable, so I need to prepare you for these challenges and coach you to face them. In turn, you'll do this for your team members as you strive for superior excellence."

(Glenn)

"How can I improve my leadership to move from where it is today to superior?"

(Coach Rusty)

"The greatest leaders never stop learning—that's what sets them apart and makes them even more impactful over time. And that's exactly what you're doing. Leadership is often about constantly refining how you show up, finding smarter, more effective ways to guide your team, and creating the conditions for them to succeed. When you focus on growth, you're not just leading—you're empowering your team to reach the

goals that matter most. You've already proven yourself to be an effective leader. Now, it's a matter of building relationships and being open to creative ideas, different solutions, and new possibilities with your team members.

"I want us to focus on what I refer to as 'The 3 Cons': Contribute, Consistency, and Confidence. These '3 Cons' are positive and necessary for leaders to help enhance each team member's commitment and experience with the team. When this happens, trust and loyalty become deeper, and team excellence becomes higher.

"Contributing means that team members want to feel that they're making a difference. It's very special to be part of a team, and everyone wants to feel like they matter and that what they're doing is important and impactful. It's the leader's responsibility to share with each team member how important their role is in order for the team to achieve its goals.

"The second 'Con' is consistency. There are two kinds of consistency that matter in leadership. The first is consistency in performance—both from the coach and the team—which drives higher productivity and stronger results. My team wanted to see that my actions matched my words, and your team would expect the same from you. They need to know that when you say you'll do something,

you'll follow through, which adds to your reliability and trustworthiness.

"The second part of consistency is following up with your team members. A strong leader consistently holds follow-up meetings with team members to support their personal growth—helping them build on their strengths and make progress in their areas of weakness. When leaders consistently deliver messages that align with their behaviors, it allows team members to understand expectations, values, and goals more clearly, which enables better coordination, collaboration, and decision-making.

"Once your team members know how they're contributing and you've established consistency, you can build their confidence, which leads to empowerment. The third 'Con'—confidence—helps team members recognize their strengths and feel supported. As a leader, it's your job to point out what they're doing well and remind them of the value they bring to the team. When individuals feel confident in their abilities, they will be more willing to step up and take responsibility for their work—so focus on these '3 Cons.'"

(Glenn)

"As leaders, we're often faced with tough situations where we can't share every detail—some things must

remain confidential. So the real challenge becomes this: how do you communicate clearly and honestly with your team, even when you can't tell them everything?"

(Coach Rusty)

"It's true that some situations need to be kept confidential. It's similar to an attorney-client privilege because the other person trusts you not to share sensitive things publicly. As much as possible, it's important to share what you can to provide clarity without violating the trust in any way. Beyond this, it's always best when you can honestly share with your team what you're thinking and feeling.

"With that in mind, let's focus on what I call 'The 4 Misses.' I've found that most problems in life happen because of Miscommunication, Misunderstanding, Misperception, and Misinformation. I want you to be proactive in avoiding the '4 Misses' because if you're not, you risk damaging relationships with your team or clients—sometimes in ways that can't be fully repaired. Let me quickly explain what I mean by these '4 Misses.'

"Miscommunication occurs when the intended message is not effectively conveyed or received. A lack of clarity can lead to conflicts, confusion, and misunderstandings.

Delivering your messages accurately and actively seeking feedback ensures that the recipient fully understands and comprehends the communication.

"Misunderstandings happen when the meaning behind a message is interpreted differently than intended and often arise due to differences in context, perspectives, and knowledge. This breakdown can lead to faulty assumptions and the misinterpretation of information. Asking questions and restating information in one's own words can help bridge these unfortunate gaps in understanding and maintain alignment with your goals.

"Misperceptions occur when we form inaccurate or incorrect beliefs about a situation, concept, or person. Sometimes, we might hear a partial communication or third-party conversation that leads us to believe something that does not match reality or the correct intent. So, it's important to be aware of this and not jump to inaccurate conclusions. Misinformation refers to misleading or false information that can lead to misguided actions or decisions. Some people might even share partial truths or take things out of context on purpose.

"Another factor is the abundance of viral content and unverified sources in today's digital landscape. Because

of this, it's crucial to take time to gather all the factual information and to separate truth from fiction.

"While there will be times when you can't share everything about a sensitive situation, being proactive in avoiding the '4 Misses' will build trust and respect with your team members. They will know that they can come to you with various issues, and you'll be able to help them because of your awareness and discretion, keeping your team moving forward."

(Glenn)

"How do I develop the full potential of the team I work with so that we can go from good to superior?"

(Coach Rusty)

"This is a loaded question, Glenn! Developing the full potential of your team requires focusing on three areas: eliminating unforced errors, performance goals, and the '6 Keys for Peak Performance.' I focus on these three areas when I'm coaching business and sports teams, and I have extreme confidence that you can do the same with your team because of the solid foundation you've already built with them.

"I define unforced errors as mistakes committed by a team that are not a direct result of the opponent's (or another person's) actions. It is the result of one's own mistakes made by an individual or organization without external pressure or influence. In other words, it's situations that you are 100 percent in control of. In tennis, I'd often say that we need to take care of business on our side of the net. Of course, we'll be aware of what our opponent is doing, but what's most important is what we do. So, focus on things that you have 100 percent control of.

"To reach a team's or individual's full potential, performance goals are essential. Everyone I know wants to win at everything they're pursuing—to reach their goals. I don't know anyone that likes losing. But what influences winning, making money, achieving goals, or developing your team's full potential? It's your performance. It's what you do that determines whether or not you achieve your desired result. So, performance goals focus on the process of achieving success rather than just the outcome. This means that individuals who set performance goals are more likely to focus on the actions and behaviors necessary to achieve their goals rather than being fixated on the end result.

"I explain the '6 Keys for Peak Performance' in great detail in my third book, Superior. *The 6 keys are physical,*

mental, emotional, strategical, tactical, and environmental. When a team is able to execute all six keys at the highest levels, peak performance happens. And it doesn't happen sometimes—it will happen all the time. So, when individuals and teams commit to eliminating unforced errors, executing performance goals, and mastering the '6 Keys for Peak Performance,' it will lead to the development of their full potential in business and sports."

(Glenn)

"How can I assure that the organization I lead will be able to sustain success for generations to come?"

(Coach Rusty)

"Glenn, this is a fantastic position to be in. There are two types of situations that organizations are striving for: They are climbing the mountain to achieve success or defending the mountain to sustain success. When you're striving to sustain success, you've established solid foundations within your organization across the board, including teamwork, open and honest communication, moral character, accountability, disciplined details, and a victor mindset—and having read Superior, *you know that I specifically share the '8 Keys for Sustaining Success.'*

I'm extremely confident that incorporating my system of building a superior culture of excellence by committing to these 8 Keys will ensure any organization sustained success, including yours.

"Knowing that you're in the process of integrating these 8 Keys, I want us to focus on my concept of high achievers versus superior achievers. I love coaching people to become high achievers, and once they do, I want to coach them to become superior achievers. Let me explain this in detail.

"Both high achievers and superior achievers possess a drive for accomplishment and success, but the two have distinct differences. High achievers are disciplined, consistently perform above average, and excel in their endeavors. They are goal-oriented, work diligently to meet and exceed expectations, and strive to continuously improve their skills and performance.

"On the other hand, superior achievers go beyond high achievement and consistently demonstrate exceptional performance and surpass the standards set by high achievers. They set themselves apart by their ability to lead, innovate, and make a significant impact in their chosen areas.

"Superior achievers possess a unique combination of qualities, such as visionary thinking, creativity, work ethic, and the ability to inspire and influence others. They are

also driven by intrinsic motivation and a deep passion for their work, and they consistently push boundaries and redefine what is possible.

"I mention this because you are a superior achiever. Remember, I always say that everything starts with the CEO or Head Coach. In addition to reinforcing the '8 Keys for Sustaining Success,' developing as many high achievers within your organization as possible is imperative. Once you do, you'll need to inspire them to become superior achievers. This is vital because they will become mentors to others and repeat what you have done for them.

"When you can add the element of multiplication in this way by having role models who mirror your same values, principles, and disciplines, along with the '8 Keys,' you will solidify your legacy and assure long-term success for your organization."

In conclusion, it is my hope that you enjoyed being a spectator in this process and learned something you can take with you in your life journey because no matter what our occupations are, in a sense, we are all leaders. Some of us are leaders within our homes. Some of us are leaders at work. Some of us are leaders of athletic teams. Many of us lead in various capacities by taking on multiple leadership roles. I pray that this book will help you become the leader you wish to be. If this book accomplishes that one goal, it will be worth every minute I spent writing it.

Our family's favorite vacation spot is Disneyland.

Charles Moura Held Many

My grandfather was a "Luna" or manager on the plantation, but also spent his free time writing songs and poems.

During my early years, it was funny to see myself featured in teen magazines.

Over time, my hard work in the music industry was recognized with various awards.

My happiest moments on the road were with my good friend Elsa.

My first performance on stage with my lifelong friend, Pali.

Mr. Meister was the inspiration behind me becoming an educator and singer.

Mr. Sakimai was one of the earliest people in my life who believed in me.

One of the most amazing educational experiences in my life was learning at Oxford University.

Tennis is more than a sport for me; it's a passion.

My managers, Lenny and Larry Silver, treated me as family.

My favorite teacher in high school!

Jay Stone is solely responsible for my recording "Nothing's Gonna Change My Love for You" and for successfully starting my professional career as a singer.

I was lucky enough to see the Berlin Wall both before and after its fall.

The legendary comedian Frank Delima was a mentor to me, and the popular radio personality Sweetie Pacarro eventually became a board member of Saint Louis School.

A brilliant man and my favorite professor in college.

As you can see, my story about Jose and our tour bus is 100 percent true!

Although I missed much of my high school years being on tour, I will always remember the moments I did spend with my classmates.

What an honor it was to be invited to sing for the President of Portugal, Mario Soares.

One of my greatest honors was being chosen as the commencement speaker at my alma mater.

ACKNOWLEDGMENTS

Thank you, Lord, for inspiring me to write this book to help others learn from my successes and mistakes in life. Everyone has an extraordinary memoir to write about their respective lives, but the reality of actually completing one requires help from many individuals and groups. I want to take this opportunity to express my gratitude to those people.

From my amazing wife and children to my loving mother, brother, two sisters, and my best friend Dr. Wynn Okua, thank you for your encouragement throughout the process. Secondly, I would like to extend mahalo to my publishers, Bryan Heathman and Alice Kirkwood, who guided me through a process I had never experienced before with great care and sensitivity. Also, I would like to thank my leadership coach, Rusty Komori, who not only imparted a wealth of wisdom to me but also provided guidance as I wrote the book, having written several himself.

As I wrote this memoir, there were moments when I felt the need to be alone, setting aside all my work-related tasks and focusing solely on writing. Just in time, Robin and Lilian Yoshimura kindly offered me the use of a place to get this done on weekends. In addition, I would like to thank the Marianists who consistently encouraged me to complete this book, doing everything they could to support me with prayers, advice, and more. In particular, I would like to extend my mahalo to Brother John Campbell, who has been an incredible mentor to me.

Finally, Dr. Lawrence Tseu and the late Dr. John Henry Felix provided me the opportunity to travel to Oxford, England, to focus on completing this memoir at Oxford University. The experience was one I will never forget. The many hours I spent writing there were invaluable.

ABOUT THE AUTHOR

Glenn Medeiros is an American singer, songwriter, and educator best known for his hit singles. Born in Hawaii, Glenn gained global attention as a teenager with the release of his debut single, "Nothing's Gonna Change My Love for You." Eight albums later, Glenn's music achieved a #1 position on the Billboard Hot 100, sold seven million records, and included collaborations with Bobby Brown and French actress/singer Elsa Lunghini.

Medeiros became an educator in his twenties. While teaching, he earned a doctorate in Educational Leadership from the University of Southern California.

Soon after, he became the president of Saint Louis School in Honolulu.

Beyond music and education, Glenn is known for his work in the community, serving as a board member in various non-profit organizations in Hawaii to support local initiatives.